100 YEARS OF THE EVENING Herald

James Mildren

BOSSINEY BOOKS

First published in 1994
by Bossiney Books, St Teath, Bodmin, Cornwall.

Printed by Penwell Ltd, Callington, Cornwall.

ISBN 0948158 98 0

ACKNOWLEDGEMENTS
Front cover design: MAGGIE GINGER

JAMES Mildren, who lives at Morice Town, Devonport, is one of the most respected journalists in the Westcountry today. Formerly on the staff of the **Western Morning News**, he retired from full-time journalism in 1988 and now works as a freelance writer and broadcaster. This is James Mildren's fifth title for Bossiney. His **Castles of Devon** remains in print, and now in **100 Years of the Evening Herald** he recalls some of the great news stories. As he says '... some century, some news!' Words and wonderful old photographs show how and why the **Herald** has become such 'a trusted and reliable family friend.'

THE PAPER that caught the mood of the times – the first edition of the Western Evening Herald.

100 Years of The Evening Herald

THE *Evening Herald* has become a trusted and reliable family friend to several generations of readers. I have been a lifelong subscriber and admirer of the paper – as well as contributing to its columns as a journalist. Writing this book has made me acutely aware of how distinctively the *Herald* has chronicled the story of Plymouth and surrounding districts: it has also helped fight their battles against injustices. One day, I hope, someone will compile an index to the complete *Herald*: that would open up a century and more of local history to those who love and benefit from such exploration. My chosen extracts merely graze the edges of a century of news. But some century: and some news!

Let us begin with this newspaper of ours on a wet Monday in the Plymouth of April 22, 1895. At 2 pm that day, the *Herald* emerged dramatically onto the streets. Its proprietors also owned *The Daily Western Mercury*, a morning newspaper of 'independent and undeviating Liberal principles'. The rival *Western Morning News* was shocked: the production of the *Evening Herald* had been one of Plymouth's best-kept secrets. The opposition geared itself to repulse the newcomer: too late, the *Herald* caught the mood of the times and never relaxed its grip.

The *Mercury*'s owner, the Launceston MP, Thomas Owen, and his manager, James Kerry, had foreseen the need for an evening newspaper in 1893 when a serious accident happened outside King Street Wesleyan Church, and the public had to wait until the following morning to learn the details. The first edition, announced on placards and handbills only hours before its appearance, was printed on buff-coloured paper. Fading, fragile original copies still exist in the Plymouth public library. Later, green paper was used for the main teatime editions – and even pink for special 'war' issues. Street vendors persisted in calling it the 'Green 'Erald' long after it was printed on conventional white paper.

Plymouth knows the mutability of war. Coverage of the Jameson Raid during the Boer War helped the *Herald* circulation soar. Sales of the 'Ladysmith Day' issue are said to have exceeded 100,000 copies, and added a regular 10,000 to daily circulation.

Despite the proprietor's Liberal tradition, the *Herald* followed a doggedly independent political line. Its appeal lay in the fast news service, topicality and exceptionally well-informed local gossip columns such as 'On The Watch in the West', 'Talk of the City' and 'Citizen's Diary.' The *Herald* supported womens' interests and was dedicated to sports reporting. Yet, by April, 1921, the *Mercury* group, of which the *Herald* was an integral part, faced financial crisis.

Sir Leicester Harmsworth, brother of the Press tycoon Lord Northcliffe, had already snapped up the *Western Morning News*. He now acquired the troubled *Mercury* and its sister-paper, the *Herald*. A revitalised *Western Morning News* emerged with the *Herald* as its profitable companion. The *Mercury* vanished. The *Herald*'s founding editors, the incomparable RAJ Walling, and his close colleague, JJ Judge, switched jobs and allegiance to the *Sunday Western Independent*, and to its owners, the Astors. The *Herald* bedded down amicably with the *Morning News*, sharing reporters, photographers, offices and machinery.

It boomed during the 1930s. There were several 'Sunday' editions dealing with such sensations as the mutiny at Dartmoor Prison. Walling and Judge had gone, but the sociable W Owen Mills, whose sharply-observed Citizen's Diary reports flush out the Plymouth society of the inter-War years, encouraged CW Bracken to serialise a history of Plymouth in the *Herald*. The newspaper, however, marketed its conscience as well as its memory. Its involvement in community affairs had been pioneered by J J Judge, a founder member of the Plymouth Guild of Social Service. The newspaper launched an 'Empty Stocking Fund' for needy children, and campaigned for improvements to maternity, child welfare and social work in Plymouth and Cornwall. Between 1936 and 1938, Leicester Harmsworth House arose on the original *Mercury-Herald* site in Frankfort Street. It survived the Blitz and emerged like a sanctuary amid the post-war architectural wilderness of straight lines in the new Plymouth. But The Three Towns had been insanitary and chronically overcrowded, an evil not altogether abolished before 1941 when the force-majeure of a blitz left no room for political compromise. The subsequent vision and vitality of Plymouth in the decade from 1945 are reflected brilliantly in the pages of the rejuvenated *Herald* of that period. The Abercrombie-Paton Watson plans were made substance. One Lord Mayor, Harry Taylor, put Plymouth's post-War mood into perspective, unforgettably, when he said: 'We pray not only to have a city beautiful to behold, but a city with a soul.'

Between 1960 and 1980 the *Herald* chronicled the reconstruction of the city centre, the expanse of housing into green field sites, and the growing diversity of 'alternative' industry. The 1980s brought recession, increasing unemployment and crime, and a growing threat to the Dockyard's position from the Cold-War 'Peace' dividend. In 1987, the *Herald* went 'tabloid' in appearance, but thankfully, not tone. Even as it prepared to set down new roots in a flagship building at Derriford, it won an award as Britain's Community Newspaper of the Year by exhorting Plymouth to 'Wake Up!'. Without losing its impartiality, the paper has enjoyed long (if occasionally exasperating) love affairs with Plymouth Argyle, Devonport Dockyard and the Armed Services. Never, though, has it ceased to champion Westcountry and, in particular, Plymouth's causes. What would one give to be able to write the story of its second century!

The Editors of the *Evening Herald* have been:

R A J Walling (1895 – 1904); J J Judge (1904 – 1922); W Owen Mills (1922 – 1940); John Collins (1940 – 1951); J B Paterson (1951 – 1967); Geoff Irish (1967 – 1979); Jim Mitchell (1979 – 1984); Alan Goode (1984 – 1988); Alan Cooper (1988 –).

The author is especially grateful to John Elliott and the staff of the Plymouth Library; to Jenny Lee and her staff at the *Evening Herald* Library; to Paul Brough of West Devon Records Office; to Alan Cooper, Editor, and Tony Carney, picture editor, of the *Evening Herald*; and to that fount of local knowledge, Crispin Gill – distinguished fellow labourer.

James Mildren
Devonport
September 1994

LAYING the foundation stone of the city museum (1897) with masonic ritual. It became a ▶ showpiece for displaying such treasures as the Winstanley Lighthouse Salt, or the 1721 copy of the Plymouth Weekly journal.

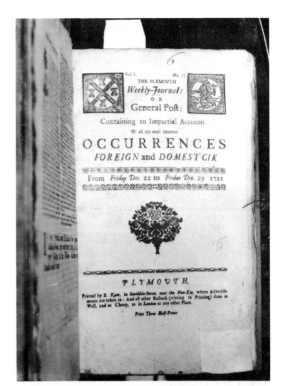

1895

The *Herald*'s first leader comment was precise and practical. 'The lack of a good evening paper has long been a lamentable hiatus in the social and communal life of the West of England. 'The *Western Evening Herald*' steps into the breach ... our programme is very simple. It is to give the news of the day in the most readable form ... to provide our supporters with the best halfpennyworth of reading matter that can be produced.'

Advertisements – mainly small ads, a specialty of the *Herald* – dominated the front page of all three editions: the *Herald*'s other strength, local news, filled the remainder of the columns sprawled throughout its broad pages.

There was tragedy in the Hamoaze. In a strong south-easterly wind, a six-oared gig capsized. Two men, both members of Devonport YMCA, drowned. It was the first major news story. A dense fog prevailed in the Channel; the Continent was cut off: but the *Herald* was a runaway success.

'Today's print will be much bigger,' promised the overwhelmed proprietors, who candidly admitted that its reception had been, 'far more cordial than even ourselves had expected.'

That **April** the 5,600-ton cruiser, Talbot, and the 1,050-ton sloop, Phoenix, were launched at Devonport: it made a brilliant spectacle.

Popham, Radford & Co were offering bedroom suites from £3 12s 6d; sideboards from £4 12s. For 72/6 (£3.62) inclusive, customers could purchase a full-size black and brass bedstead, spring mattress, wool mattress, feather bolster and two feather pillows. Mr T Bowen's list of properties for sale included a well-built 12-room house on Plymouth Hoe at £950, or a compact six-room house for £285.

In **May**, at Tavistock, a new Grammar School was opened in Plymouth Road: the Duke of Bedford donated £20,000 towards its cost. In the Oscar Wilde trial, the jury split 9 to 3: a re-trial was ordered. Sensational stuff.

Fire, in Union Street, Plymouth, destroyed Mr Roach's steam slate and marble works. When the inferno threatened neighbouring buildings, 'the minute gun from Mount Wise was sounded in the Garrison. The detachment of the Berkshire Regiment responded. Captain Burns of the Devonport reel also put in an appearance.'

Damage was estimated at £4,000; the building was insured for £2,000. Within 24-hours there was another fire, at James and Rosewall's lead, paint, oil and brass manufactury in Octagon Street. Again, the minute gun was fired: on this occasion the Royal Marines came to the rescue.

At Burrator, a deep trench was being excavated for the Sheepstor Dam. It was 700-feet long and 78-feet deep at the sump-hole. The Duke of Cambridge inspected troops at Devonport Brickfields: 'He bestrode a magnificent black horse ... bayonets flashed in the sunlight ... red coats glowed ... music was not wanting ... then a tiny dog strolled casually on to the ground and dignity was invaded by impudence.'

In **June**, the rain fell like a water curtain. In mid-**July**, Devon and Cornwall went to the polls. The *Herald* produced hourly 'Extras' up-dating the results. Electoral passion was intense. Carriages whirled in all directions through Plymouth's narrow streets. 'Irish Home Rule is dead,' proclaimed the Herald. The Conservatives and Unionists, under Salisbury, had triumphed.

1896

The New Year headline was explosive: 'War Probable'. The South African conflict involved 'kith and kin'. Westcountrymen had emigrated to South Africa in large numbers. Now the Boers were on the offensive.

The *Herald* reported, on **January 11**, that:

'A large number of all grades in Devonport Dockyard were informed that they would be required to work until 8 p.m. tonight on the Hermione and six torpedo destroyers to be commissioned on Tuesday, in addition to the 1,000 and more hands who have been working nightly until 9 p.m. for some weeks now.'

The British Fleet in the Channel was the strongest in our history with 60,000 men and 400 guns: there were six of the most powerful battleships afloat, the Majestic, Magnificent, Royal Sovereign, Empress of India, Repulse and Resolution, all exceeding 14,000-tons, as well as two 9,000-ton cruisers and seven smaller ships.

In **February**, Cecil Rhodes landed at Plymouth from the Union Steamship, Moor. He refused to be interviewed. Having spent a short time at the Grand Hotel, he entrained from Millbay Station. On **February 15** the Devonport Dockyard extension began at Keyham. Employees of Sir John Jackson & Co began constructing a new road from Ford Creek to Camel's Head. It was the start of a huge investment.

The *Herald*'s headline, 'Disaster and Wholesale Emigration Feared' in its Cornish edition revealed potential financial calamity. Michael Henry Williams was threatening to sell his major shareholding in Cornish mines.

THE MUCH-LOVED Royal Albert Hospital (1862 – 1982) supported for years by the voluntary effort of the local community through Hospital Saturdays and other fund-raising events.

EM BARRY's handsome RNE College (1897 – 1986) at Keyham. The building survived the blitz, but not the MoD management accountants.

Even the Boer problem was relegated to the background. In **June**, there was cricket at Mount Wise; Compton Giffard was amalgamated into 'Greater Plymouth'; the C-in-C, Plymouth, directed that white cap covers and white trousers be worn by sailors, 'during the present tropical weather': and, at Barras Nose, North Cornwall, the newly-formed National Trust pleaded for donations to buy its very first coastal holding of 14 acres.

The *Herald* was serialising popular books; 'Revelations of a Doctor', and 'Madam of the Ivies'. There were now five editions daily, the fifth and final at 5.45 pm. They contained no photographs, only simple line sketches. Weather 'forecasts', comprised 'reports and predictions' made by Mr H Victor Prigg, the borough meteorologist. His readings were taken at the Met Station on Plymouth Hoe.

That **December**, a 2,000-ton steamer, the Aerial, became embedded on rocks at the foot of the Citadel. It had parted with its anchor cable. The *Herald* reported: 'The remarkable feature of the gale was the suddenness with which it developed severity. The sea in the Sound was almost unprecedentedly violent, and the large vessel went ashore under the Hoe. Four crew are reported missing.' The Aerial had steamed around the Sound, sending up distress signals, and blowing for assistance, in full view of hundreds of spectators attracted by the firing of rockets. Fortunately, the missing crew members turned up at the Sailors' Home in Vauxhall Street.

In court, a gipsy was charged with fortune-telling, for 'witching' a woman who refused to buy a dozen lucky clothes-pegs. She received two months imprisonment with hard labour.

1897

June – the Diamond Jubilee. The Queen, 'Radiant and serene turns her head from side to side to face her loyal and enthusiastic subjects. Oh! God Save the Queen! Not a throat is mute, not an eye but kindles. She is with us. There she sits, the beloved sovereign. The great, good Queen Victoria.'

'Plymouth, almost more than any other town, is in the matter of population, almost a creation of the Queen's reign. The development of trade and the development of the dockyard works at Devonport have both been remarkable … If the 2,000-odd inhabitants entertained yesterday by the Mayor could have been transported to other soil in 1837, and have returned in 1897, they would certainly not have been able to recognise the place … but on the whole, improvements have been vastly beneficial to the community.'

In Plymouth, the Mayor laid the foundation stone of the Museum and Art Gallery … a prominent Freemason, he was heard to say that, 'as a poor mason, I have done my level best.' On the Hoe, flames from a 175-ton monster bonfire curled around Smeaton Tower. Houses in Plympton St Maurice were wreathed in masses of green laden branches and wild flowers. On Sheepstor, a great fire stack was guarded by an old man and his dog from the 'brand of the mischievous … all around was a sea of mist, with billows of clouds. The pretty little Princetown fire engine was decorated with flags and laurel and foxgloves.'

At Devonport, the Mayor laid the founda-

A DEVONPORT roofscape outside the Dockyard walls: overcrowding was endemic in the huddle of houses.

tion stone of a new Technical School near the South Western Railway Station. Then some 2,200 adults and children 'partook of a feast prepared for them at the expense of Mr H.E. Kearley M.P … an abundance of boiled and roast beef, ham, beef pies, plum pudding and boiled potatoes, and the vast crowd of Devonport's poor went away highly delighted. The blaze in Devonport Park was built up of 300 tar barrels and tons of other material.'

In Stonehouse, the chairman of the District Council wore a new chain of office when he opened the pleasure grounds, Victoria Gardens, given by the Lord of the Manor, Lord Mount Edgcumbe. The feu de joie: 'Spectators on the Hoe could see the line of fire begin on the brow of the hill above Picklecombe Fort, flash among the woods of Mount Edgcumbe, across the grassy slopes of Cremyll as fast as lighting: in a few seconds it has reached Longroom, and the rattle grows louder and louder, and suddenly, the whole line of soldiers on the Hoe were firing, the crack of rifles deafened the ears, and the smell of gunpowder assailed the nerves, and then the firing passed across the front of the Citadel and down to the water's edge. It was taken up at Batten, and the thin red line, stretching up the hillside to the great wall at Staddon responded … then the cannons were fired again, and the whole operation was performed three times. The line could not have been less than nine miles long, the men were placed three paces apart – soldiers, Marines and volunteers, from Picklecombe Fort to Bovisand Fort.'

1898

August – 'The *Western Daily Mercury* and The *Western Evening Herald* have a larger circulation than any other two papers in the West of England … ONE MILLION COPIES A MONTH.'

September – The great exodus from Plymouth to Burrator was by train and bicycle. The traffic at Dousland was thick as that in the Strand. The great dam which has taken five years to build, is one of the largest in England '… the most coveted view was the road crowning it at the top over the arches which is to take the place of the old lane to Sheepstor.'

The day after Burrator reservoir's opening, Devonport ratepayers again called for the 'municipalisation' of their supply. A typical annual water rate was 30/- (£1.50).

There were 23 cases of typhoid at Honicknowle (pop. 206): 'No wonder,' exploded the *Herald*, 'polluted atmosphere, polluted water and a fever-stricken village.' An obnoxious odour pervaded from a grossly polluted stream, an open cesspit and a manure farm.

What did Victorians consider to be the most marvellous invention of the Queen's reign? The electric telegraph; the sewing machine; the telephone; the X-ray? Ranking above these was Thomas Alva Edison's invention, the phonograph; 'a bit of glass in a frame, a bit of sapphire, a waxen cylinder, a machine that revolves by clockwork and a tin horn. That evanescent thing, the human voice, has been caught, and made to repeat itself for all time!'

1899

Barnum and Bailey's circus visited Plymouth: 'Some enthusiasts got up almost before they went to bed to witness the entry of the four great trains (at Friary Station) and the deportation of the show to the ground at Pennycomequick.'

Henry Debeig, a hawker, exposed his feet in Union Street, 'so he might get something from any charitable person.' A police officer said the man suffered from very bad feet. So bad, that the authorities refused him entry to the Workhouse.

The Number Six green (tram) car was proceeding down North Hill to Mutley Plain when the horses, pulling back, the pole broke and the pin came out. The frightened animals ran away from the car with the pole clattering behind them.

In Truro, the Australian touring side played an England XI. The visitors made 214; the 'immortal' Victor Trumper, then on his first tour, scored 19 and Darling, a fighting 55. England were dismissed for 87: their skipper, the great R E Foster, made 16 not out: the fast-bowler, E Jones took 7 for 31. England followed on and were all out for 192, L C Braund making 63. The 'Colonials' won by eight wickets.

That year died Sir William H White. Born in 1845 in James Street, Devonport, the son of a local currier, White rose to become Director of Naval Construction. He replaced the 'wooden walls of Old England' with iron and steel-armoured vessels of enormous power – a re-incarnation of John Hawkyns.

1900

'The gathering which assembled in Plymouth Guildhall-square last night to see the old year out and the new year in was not much different to those which have disturbed the peace on similar occasions on the same spot ever since it has been a public space. Few troubled themselves with the fin-de-siecle controversy. Of the popular songs sung, 'The Miner's Dream' was favourite. The crowd, at 12, must have embraced several thousand people. As the bells pealed in 1900, a white flare was lighted and an attempt made to sing Auld Lang Syne. A marvellous variety of keys and lack of sustained effort made it a dismal failure.'

February – A Boer War Report: 'A thrill of pleasure will go through Devonians when receiving the pleasurable news. Well dune (sic) Devons, well dune indeed!...We can imagine the yell they let loose when the order was given: Fix bayonets! Charge! Such a yell as the merry pirates of Drake used to give as they poured down on some luckless Spaniard; first to crest Elandslaaghte Hill; ahead of a thousand heroes in that wild rush

to death and glory; and victors of Saturday's bloody struggle. Sons of the soil are they, children of the waving fields and sweet pastures of dear Devonia.'

On **February 8**, the Plymouth Conservative 'Seven Hundred' passed a resolution as a result of which (reported the *Herald*) Sir Edward Clarke may resign his seat. Clarke had vigorously attacked his Party, including Chamberlain, the Colonial Minister, on the conduct of the Boer War, and called for his dismissal. Enraged Plymouth Conservatives met in private, banned reporters, and demanded that Clarke resign his seat. The Barrister, one of the most distinguished men to serve Plymouth during the 19th century, resigned, and applied to the Chancellor of the Exchequer for the Chiltern Hundreds.

The *Western Evening Herald* sold out over and over again on **March 1** when, in mid-morning, it was first to announce the relief of Ladysmith. A plain, single-column headline said it all: 'Ladysmith Relieved. Lord Dundonald Entered the Town Last Night. Flight of the Boers. The news reached us about 10.15 and the '*Herald*' boys were supplying an eager public with our Special before eleven. Outside our offices, large numbers of people gathered and gave vocal evidence of their pleasure.'

The sufferings of the Garrison (numbering about 12,000) had been terrible. The siege lasted from November 2 until February 28 - 119 days. Ladysmith was filth-polluted, with fever, dysentery and diarrhoea rife – Not even the water from the River Klip could be boiled on account of the scarcity of fuel, and was thick with animal matter. The men were reduced to eating horseflesh: they were rationed to a little bread and biscuit, an ounce of sugar and an ounce of tea. The once dashing Calvary Brigade had ceased to exist. The poor emaciated mere phantoms of horses were among the most painful sights of the whole siege.

1901

January 1 – 'Some people are endeavouring cynically to deprive us of the little thrill which affords for the birth of an Epoch. They say that it is all folly. Dionysus Exiguus made a mistake in the calendar and put the commencement of the Christian era four years later than it really should have been. Thus today is really January 1, 1905!'

Thick black rules separated the columns of news in the Memorial Edition of **January 23** – 'The first intimation of the mournful event was a telegram from the Prince of Wales to the Lord Mayor dated Osborne, 6.45 p.m. – My beloved Mother, the Queen, has just passed away surrounded by her children and grandchildren. - Albert Edward.

'All Monday night the Queen lay in her bedroom in the pavilion in a very restless state. It was locked, the only persons allowed within being the doctors, the dressers, and two maid who were under the superintendence of Nurse Soal from the sanatorium on the Estate. The end came at half-past six. It was absolutely peaceful and painless and the Queen breathed her last in the presence of her children and grandchildren, of the Bishop of Winchester, and the Lord Chamberlain (the Earl of Clarendon) who arrived just in time. The gates are closed, and no messages have come from the house of death.'

'At the Devonport Dockyard and other Government establishments, the Royal Standard floats at half-mast. At Noon, H.M.S. Nile and other ships fired 81 guns. The meaning of the 81 guns are one for each completed year of the Queen's age.'

On **March 29** at the Plymouth Magistrates Court, a hawker, summoned by the RSPCA for cruelty, was ordered to have his horse destroyed forthwith. Two days later, the same hawker was back in court: far from having the poor animal destroyed, he'd sold it for 10 shillings to a gipsy. He was fined 20 shillings.

The King, the Edwardians were told, 'has given an order for his third motor-car.'

On **December 12** at Tavistock, the extensive and delightfully- situated residence known as Abbotsfield, with 6 acres of pleasure gardens and grounds was sold to Mr E C Rundle, the Duke of Bedford's steward, acting on behalf of the Duke, for £655.

And in an Extra Special, on **Monday, December 16**, the *Western Evening Herald* reported 'Marconi's Triumph – Wireless Wires Between Cornwall and America – Scientific Men Amazed. On Wednesday and Thursday of last week Marconi conducted secret experiments between St John's, Newfoundland and Poljew, Cornwall, and in three hours time he received from the English station three dots, which in the Marconicode make the letter S … the receiving apparatus at St John's consisted of a kite sent 400 feet up into the air, to which was attached a Marconi receiving rod connected by a cable with a machine on the earth … so confident is he of almost immediate success that he had made arrangements to send a New York newspaper an account of King Edward's coronation by wireless telegraphy.'

1902

June 2 – The Boer War ends: 'In Plymouth, there was a general atmosphere of rejoicing. The war has lasted 2 years, 7 months and 20 days. There is solid pleasure in the knowledge that the weary struggle is at an end. There is no mafficking. There are more than 20,000 British graves in South Africa.'

In the Three Towns, 'cheap houses' were for sale. Mortgage interest was at $3\frac{1}{2}$ %. For £26 per annum, it was possible to rent a smart 8-roomed house in up-market Mannamead. Lower down the scale, £15 per annum secured a four-roomed terraced cottage in Laira.

June 25 – 'The King's malady, perityphlitis, is said to have made a definite appearance nine days ago. It was hoped to avoid an operation till after the Coronation. Although the little sac called the appendix, the utility of which in the human constitution is unknown, is on the right front, the pain caused by its inflammation is felt just above the umbilical depression, and this is the first aid to accurate diagnosis. An abscess had formed which blocked the natural channel, and would have involved certain death if not speedily removed. The King submitted himself with singular courage to the operation. The incision was made near the groin, and was carried upwards with an outer slant for close on four inches. Such operations invariably involve considerable risk, notwithstanding the strides made by modern surgery ... the operation was discovered by Sir Frederick Treves who operated upon the King.'

1903

January – 'Major Pringle, R.E., of the Board of Trade, this morning inspected the new extension of the Plymouth Corporation Tramways from Hyde Park to Peverell Park ... the service to Peverell will be a 12 minute one from the Theatre.'

The population of the Three Towns in 1903 was – Plymouth 107,636; Devonport 70,437 and Stonehouse 15,111 – total 193,184. A letter to the *Western Evening Herald* argued that if the Three Towns employed only one Town Clerk (instead of three) the saving in his salary alone would be £1,000 per annum ...

'Enormous damage was done by the fire which broke out at the Great Western Docks, Plymouth, last night. The engineering works of Messrs Bickle, where the fire commenced, and the huge saw mills adjoining, belonging to Messrs Jewson, were destroyed ... half an acre of ground was soon covered by a blazing, roaring bonfire. The crews of ships were on the alert to prevent their rigging from destruction; the horses were removed from the stables of the Royal Marine Barracks. When the fire was at its height, the Government tug, Industrious, arrived, and poured two of the biggest jets of water into the fire.'

'A woman of 44 was charged with being a lunatic wandering at large in Mount-street. Dr Wolferstan found she was suffering from delusions, and that she was impelled to do things by spirits. She had been at Blackadon three times. The Bench ordered the woman to be detained at the workhouse for 14 days.'

1904

The 1903-1904 association football season saw the emergence of Plymouth Argyle as a member of the Western and the Southern Leagues. In their final match of the season they beat Reading four-nil before a crowd of 7,000 people at Home Park. The *Western Evening Herald* published a popular Football Herald, on pink paper, every Saturday during the soccer and rugby season.

May – 'The recorded times of the great run from Plymouth to Paddington yesterday are very striking reading. With a stop of four minutes at Bristol, the Great Western flier did the trip of 246 miles in 227 minutes, or 223 minutes if the stop at Bristol be eliminated. The average speed was well over 65 miles an hour. There is no doubt that the Great Western could have reduced the time to 3h 30m in a straightaway run. When they get their new route via Westbury, they will be able to do still quicker times on special occasions...boat trains will run at a more moderate schedule of about 4h 20m.'

April – 'Rear-Admiral W.H. Henderson, Superintendent of Devonport Dockyard, has had his attention drawn by the Devonport Merchantile Association to alleged irregular practices in the establishment under his command. Goose clubs, blanket and clothing clubs and sales of jewellery are conducted. There are men engaged in offices who are auditors and inspectors of Co-operative Societies, and take books into the yard in the morning, returning them in the evening...'

SUBMARINERS at the funeral of their comrades, victims of the cruel A8 calamity of 1905.

1905

June 8 – 'Another terrible submarine disaster has occurred, involving, it is feared, the loss of fifteen lives. Submarine A8 was lost a short distance outside Plymouth Breakwater this morning while on a run. At 10.20 a.m. three explosions were seen on board the vessel ... a buoy was placed on the place, and the torpedo-boat steamed into harbour for assistance. Dockyard tugs were sent out, and divers went down. Later, a violent explosion occurred below, and diving operations were stopped. There is no hope of recovering the men inside the vessel.'

June 14 – 'At 4 a.m. the unpleasant and dangerous work of removing the bodies from the submarine lying submerged to the deck in the dock was resumed ... dense fumes of gas still rose from the craft. By the time workmen entered the Dockyard at 6.45, the bodies had been removed to the electricity generating station and placed in their coffins.'

The funeral, on June 15, was 'The most remarkable from the point of view of numbers and pathetic feelings that has ever been witnessed in the Borough of Devonport. In Fore Street all the shops were closed as the mournful procession passed through ... all traffic was stopped ... there were vast crowds all along the route to the cemetery.'

There was a bizarre footnote to that terrible

16

tragedy. 'Submarines each carry three white mice, whose sensitiveness to gasoline escapes is so acute that they immediately give warning of such escapes by squealing.'

1906

October – 'A storm of great severity was very severely felt at Polperro ... soon after five o'clock, three tremendous seas were seen a great distance off shore. Travelling very rapidly they dashed in quick succession on the peak at the entrance to the harbour, and going right over hid it from view.'

'Active preparations are in progress at Devonport in connection with the laying down of a new battleship. She will presumably be of the Dreadnought class.'

'A serious tramway accident occurred on the Devonport and District Tramway this morning. The No. 14 car left the Terminus, Pennycomequick, at six o'clock for Keyham Gates. At Albert-road the driver was unable to pull up owing to the greasy state of the rails. The car gathered speed. The driver applied all brakes but failed to bring the car to a standstill. At the bottom of Albert-road, the car jumped the rails, dashed on the pavement, knocked down iron railings and came with terrific force against a huge tree, which was smashed off like a carrot. The driver, who gallantly stuck to his post, escaped serious injury, as did over 50 passengers.'

November – 'There has been another crisis in Newton Abbot Workhouse. Some of the gentleman who are in residence have revolted. The menu at dinner yesterday was suet pudding, sixteen ounces of it.'

CROWDS mill through Union Street, Plymouth.

1907

April – 'H.M.S. Trafalgar has gone ashore at Devil's Point. She was being turned down the Hamoaze by tugs when, off the Victualling Yard, she went on rocks, where she still remains.'

May – 'The foundation stone of the new elementary school at Prince Rock, Plymouth, was laid this afternoon. Since the erection of the first school in Treville-street 34 years ago, great strides have been made. In our elementary schools now there are 18,244 children, in our secondary school 635 students and in evening schools, 2,500. The authority has engaged 732 teachers.'

June – A discussion on infant mortality was the first ever held in the Three Towns. 'In the decennium ending 1906 the approximate infant mortality per 1000 births recorded at the Military Families Hospital at Devonport was 43.00; the rate among the civilian population for the same period was 134.6. The French had introduced the 'Creche' for which there could be ample work in Devonport and Stonehouse where a large number of women went out daily to work, leaving their children in the care of ignorant and dirty landladies.'

'There was an immense crowd of 6,000 in the Drill Hall to hear the Prime Minister, Sir Henry Campbell-Bannerman, attack the House of Lords for its abuse of power.'

'Mr Preston Thomas in his report says Plymouth is by far the most pauperised of the urban unions in the West of England.'

1908

Christmas Eve *Herald* bargains: A Gent's silver watch for twenty shillings from Samuel Edgecumbe the jeweller, of Cornwall Street, who allowed railway fare to all purchasers of 25 shillings value and upwards on all journeys for up to 30 miles. There were 10,000 dolls given away free at Roach's Boot Store to all who purchased goods worth 2s.11½d or more. In George Street, H. Samuel sold solid gold brooches at 2s.6d., and good timekeeping, exquisitely engraved, real gold watches for ladies at 17s.6d. Spooners & Co offered silver combs at 5s.6d. For £5.10s you could purchase a solid satin walnut bedroom suite – or for £1.9s a dining room table that would seat six. English geese were 4s to 8s (each); ducks and fowls 1/6d to 4/-; splendid little hams 1/6 to 3/- each, green or smoked; Cornish butter was 1/- a pound. Navy oak logs for Christmas fires were 6/- a quarter-ton, delivered, and a Christmas Hamper containing 6 Valencia oranges, 6 large Baldwin apples, 6 sound and yellow bananas, 1 large box Figs, 1 lb of sweet grapes, 1 lb of mixed nuts, including brazils and almonds, 1 new milky cokernut (sic), 1 lb of best sweets - the whole hamper for two shillings.

Christmas Eve – 'The Merry Motorist is to be compelled to moderate his pace to a 10-mile (an hour) limit when he drives within the boundaries of the Borough of Plymouth. At its meeting yesterday, the Watch Committee decided to apply to the Local Government Board to permit it to impose the speed limit on motor-cars. The decision will be approved by most motor-car owners. We are sure that the exhilaration of the motion of a motor is so great that drivers have to keep a watch on themselves in order to restrain their speed.'

'In the Three Towns tomorrow (January 1, 1909), there will be about 2,200 aged persons entitled to receive old-age pensions. Stonehouse has 163 or 164 claimants, where Devonport claims 804. Plymouth's 1,437 claims stand out strikingly. In Devonport, where the service element predominates, the old folk are mainly of two classes - the one in circumstances sufficiently comfortable to place them outside the pale of the Act - and the other composed of people who have long felt the pinch, and by force of sheer necessity have been compelled to seek out relief from the Guardians. Applications can be made immediately on attaining the age of 69 years and eight months ... the difficulties of discovering and verifying the ages of claimants have been very considerable largely owing to the way in which family records have been kept ... an analysis of the statistics reveals a wonderful testimony to the longevity of Plymothians: 266 of the Plymouth applicants are people of 80 or more ... a curious fact, noted in each town, is that among the females, spinsters account for less than five percent. Widows of Crimean and other war victims form the great majority.'

The Old-Age pension was graduated. Of those 'awarded' pensions in Plymouth, 1,050 old folk were paid 5 shillings a week each, while others received from 1 shilling to 4 shillings weekly. Those with yearly income in excess of £31.10s were ineligible.

1909

January – On the opening of the Plymouth Workhouse Infirmary, and new Nurses Home in Greenbank-road, the *Herald*, using one of the first photographs ever to appear in its pages reported:'Plymouth has removed a stain from its fair name. For many years its workhouse has been badly congested and, therefore, badly adapted to the most efficient administration of the Poor Law, as well as to the best treatment of the sick poor.'

January 9 – 'Mr Stephens deprecated the presence of Guardians on the Distress Committee (at a meeting of Plymouth Ratepayers Association) regarding them as the most callous and hard-hearted lot of beings he had ever seen in his life.'

January 14 – 'A Newsboys' Treat will be given in the Salvation Army Congress Hall, Martin-street, Plymouth, tonight to the newsboys of the Three Towns. The 'Herald' boys of Plymouth will march from the back of our offices in Frankfort-lane ... to the Octagon, where the Devonport lads will join, making a procession of about 700 boys (not counting the bands) to the hall.'

January 22 – The slums of Devonport were described by the vicar of St Chads, the Rev J.L. Johnson at a Three Towns Housing Association meeting. Two hundred chairs were placed out for the expected audience: 12 persons attended. 'In some of the houses he had been, they could grow cabbages on the stairs – the most beautifully-flavoured cabbages they had ever tasted (laughter). In some of the rooms both sexes lived together, which was a disgrace to Christianity and civilisation ... '

January 22 – 'Rear-Admiral Cross, Superintendent of the Dockyard at the Devonport Mercantile Association's dinner presented a picture of the town in the early part of the 18th Century when Fore-street was eight-feet wide, and Cumberland-street was 'a little path leading to Stonehouse Passage, and fit for packhorse and carts'. Ninety percent of the population of Devonport were directly or indirectly associated with the Dockyard. The physical characteristics of Devonport had changed very greatly since the 17th century when the yard was established. He quoted some details showing the number of men borne on the Dockyard books in various years. On January 1, 1904, the officers and men in the yard (including the works department but excluding the ordnance store and victualling yard) stood at 10,818. In 1905, the number was 11,207. Then came great reductions and on 1st January, 1906, the number was 8,889. But on 1st January, 1908, it had risen again to 9,670 and now stood at 10,773. The grant of money given in November to help the unemployed in the Three Towns enabled them to enter 500 men, who would be discharged on 25th March, so that the numbers in the ensuing year stood at a little over 10,000. The wages for the Dockyard going into Devonport was £61,795 per month. Devonport was getting a full share of the work of new constructions. A month from today, they intended to lay down the keel plates of the biggest cruiser the world had ever seen (applause).'

1910

January 8 – 'Mr Lloyd George (Chancellor of the Exchequer) arrived in Plymouth last evening and was met by Sir Charles Radford at Millbay and driven to the Alderman's residence in the Crescent.' He was later greeted by an immense crowd in the Drill Hall, and accorded a 2½-minute ovation.'

January 24 – 'The new comet (Halley's) was in full sight for Plymouth on Saturday evening. In the clear sky, the stars shone out with great brilliance, but were far enpassed by the splendour of Venus rising in the south-west. About five o'clock the comet appeared in the neighbourhood of the great planet … the long tail seemed to cover two degrees and was of considerable brightness.'

May 9 – 'The Admiralty yacht, Enchantress, with the Prime Minister (Asquith) aboard arrived at Plymouth. The party at once proceeded towards the special train, the Admiralty messengers eagerly purchasing copies of the *Herald* from a boy who happened to be near at hand.'

May 30 – 'King Edward made his last journey through the London he loved so well amid signs of universal grief. All heads were bared, and many tears flowed as the casket containing all that is mortal of the mighty monarch made the first stage of its journey to the grave … ' The King visited Plymouth as Prince of Wales, and Lord Steward, to open the Guildhall on August 13, 1874, and in March, 1902 to lay the keel plate of H M S. King Edward VII.

1911

Notes of the Day: 'It may well be wondered how the Three Towns ever got on without the Nursing Association and Training School for Devon and Cornwall which was started in 1906 with one staff nurse, and had today a staff of 11 and 25 pupils. During the past year 66,098 visits were paid to patients.'

Dockyard Notes: 'Not many years ago the labourers in the Dockyard were paid the miserable wage of 14 shillings a week. It is entirely due to the existence of the Government Labourers Union and the persistent agitation it has conducted in such a splendid fashion that the present minimum of a guinea has been obtained. The ambition of the organisation now is to fix the minimum at 24 shillings a week.'

December 13 – The Plymouth Justices Watch Committee resolved that the hours of licensed premises on week days be altered from 11 p.m. to 10 p.m. – that hours of opening on Sundays be limited to four hours, viz 12.30 to 2.30; 8p.m. to 10 p.m. and that clubs shall be on the same footing as licensed premises.

December 16 – 'Wireless telegraphy not being available, we cannot do more than project our minds across the boundless waste of eternal ice around the South Pole and try to make out a few tiny specks moving along it. They are the members of Captain Scott's expedition and of Captain Amundsen's, but as there is nothing to distinguish the Pole from the rest of the dazzling expanse of snow, we cannot make out whether they are going thither or returning home.'

1912

April 15 – 'The startling news was received this morning that the Titanic, the gigantic White Star liner, which left Southampton on her maiden voyage on Wednesday, collided last evening with an iceberg and sent out a wireless message asking assistance … she has a population of between 2,000 and 3,000.'

April 29 – 'Graphic stories of the Titanic disaster were related by many of the survivors of the crew of the liner, 167 of whom were landed at (The Great Western Docks) Plymouth yesterday. Large crowds gathered in the vicinity of the Dock gates to welcome the men home again. A description of the calamity was given by J Horswell, of

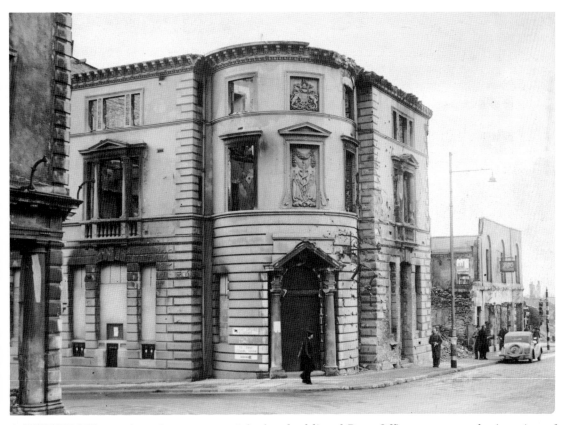

A FAVOURITE meeting place now vanished – the blitzed Post Office corner at the junction of Chapel-street and Fore-street, Devonport.

Ugborough, a sailor, one of the men who went away in an emergency boat. This boat contained only 13 people, including Sir Cosmo and Lady Duff Gordon ... he stated that on reaching the Carpathia, Sir Cosmo spontaneously expressed a wish to present each of the boat's crew with £5 to help them replace the clothes and effects they had lost.'

May 14 – 'Devon County Agricultural Show opened today under the happiest of climatic conditions. From an early hour onwards, all roads led to the eastern end of Plymouth, the excellent site at Beaumont-road being the venue of this year's show.'

June 21 – 'A petition was presented purporting to be signed by 867 shop-keepers, praying that an order should be made exempting the shop-keepers of the Borough from the operation of the compulsory half-day closing clause of the Shop Act.'

1913

April 3 – The historic Smeaton Tower on the Hoe was the object of attack of suffragettes this morning. All around the base was found painted in large white letters what was evidently intended to be a greeting to the Lords of the Admiralty (including Mr Winston Churchill) who entered the Sound on board the yacht Enchantress shortly before eight o'clock. The words, untidily, but fairly conspicuously written, were – on the Sound side: 'To Churchill: no security till you give women votes, no matter how big the Navy.'

'The Devonport gas committee recommended that the wages of five lamplighters be increased from 23 shillings to 24 shillings ... '

April 30 – 'The Lord Mayor (of London) received from the Prime Minister (H H Asquith) the following letter: 'I have carefully considered the pension to be made by the Government in accordance with the undertaken given in February last for dependents of Captain Scott and those who so heroically lost their lives in the Antarctic ... for Lady Scott, in addition to the Admiralty pension of £200 for herself and £25 per annum for her son, until he reaches the age of 18, an annuity of £100 ... for Mrs Evans, the widow of Petty Officer Evans, in addition to the Admiralty pension of 13/6d (67½ pence) weekly, a further annuity of 12/6d (62½ pence) a week, and 3/- (15 pence) a week for each of her children up to the age of 18.'

1914

January 16 – 'Submarine Disaster at Plymouth – A7 Disappears In Whitsand Bay. Submarine A7 (with two officers and nine men aboard) went down in Whitsand Bay during exercises, and she has not been seen since ... the fact that bubbles rose from her is ominous strength that water has penetrated into her.' Divers located her in 23 fathoms of water in Whitsand Bay: her stern was buried in mud, her bow pointed upwards.

January 22 – 'Seaplane No 73 arrived in Plymouth Sound at 4.40 last evening, by that time the submarine for which she had come to search had been found. The aviators maintained a height of about 100-feet: the aircraft, a bi-plane of the Morris-Farman type, came down to the surface of the water between Drake's Island and Millbay Docks, where the destroyer, Sylvia, met her.'

January 28 – 'I must argue chiefly from the point of view of war. In peace time, the augmentation of the Three Towns into three distinct bodies doesn't affect us much. The only thing I can think of is Devonport drainage which goes into the Hamoaze, and a good deal goes down by my house (laughter). The military authorities are assisted in every possible way. There are terms of great harmony and we work very well. In wartime, it becomes an entirely different question. The whole area of the Three Towns is included in the fortress in which the Fortress Commander instead of going to one authority and saying, I must have this done, has to go to three different authorities and express his views on three different occasions. The delay that might occur on a vital question at a critical moment might be very serious indeed ...' Major-General A.P. Penton, commander of South-Western Coast Defences at the eight-day long public inquiry into the amalgamation of Plymouth, Devonport and Stonehouse. Such headlines as: 'Determination of Devonport – Will Combat It to the Death' and, more subtly, 'Plymouth The Tiger: but The Lady Not Yet Inside,' dominated the *Herald*. Local issues were swept aside as a headline across eight columns on August 5 announced: 'Great Britain At War With Germany.'

August 6 – The authorities have taken over control of the two railways serving the town ... the military authorities early informed Plymouth firms owning horses that they would have to provide the Army with a number of animals. People watched with keen interest the parade of horses in the streets and the inspection by the officers making the selection ... motor wagons belonging to various local firms were also borrowed. At the request of Major-General A.P. Penton, the Fortress Commander, a representative of each of the Three Towns attended at the offices of the South-West Coast Defences. General Penton said it was his intention during the present crisis to deal with only one authority for the whole of the Three Towns. The three representatives agreed that the Mayor of Plymouth should be the representative with whom the General should deal ... excitement was heightened during the day by some unfounded rumours ... weeping women were to be seen in all parts of the towns ... '

THE HARVEST Home on the corner of Tavistock-road and Coburg-street, Plymouth – a popular pub now gone.

1915

The European conflict drove advertisements off the front-page of the *Evening Herald*. 'War' and 'Foreign' news took their place. The four-page, broadsheet newspaper was still selling at a halfpenny. The register of death from the front was appalling: the elite of a generation was being annihilated.

October 14 – 'Officers of the 3/5th Battalion, Devon Regiment, made practical use of Tavistock Goose Fair yesterday. They saw crowds of young fellows in 'civilians' about – almost as many of them as their khaki-clad brothers. A motor-car arranged with recruiting posters was driven about the streets, and the RAMC band paraded, playing popular airs ... the numbers who joined up as a result were fourteen – all well-built young fellows.'

December 28 – Notes Of The Day: 'There were few or none of the memorable incidents of Christmas 1914 about Christmas 1915 in the trenches. Too many barbarities have happened in the year to allow the men to favour an unofficial truce, foremost, probably, the villainy of the poison gas; but other memories, from the sinking of the Lusitania to the execution of Nurse Cavell, have embittered the memories of the British soldiers. Their one desire is to beat the Germans.'

December 29 – 'The Cabinet held a critical, but decisive meeting yesterday. It is understood that a majority of Ministers agreed on the recruiting question, and to introduce a means of compulsion for unmarried men ... '

1916

June 3 – The Plymouth historian, R A J Walling concluded of the Battle of Jutland that: 'No single battle in history has inflicted such loss and suffering on Plymouth.' The death-columns of the *Herald* provide a pointer to the extent of the tragedies of Jutland and of the first battle of the Somme. An eye-witness reported: 'We passed along the line of German ships some miles away. The air was heavy with masses of smoke black, yellow, green, of every colour, which drifted between the opposing lines. Again and again salvoes of shells fell far short of the mark. I watched the Iron Duke swinging through the seas, letting off broadside after broadside, wicked tongues of flame leaping through clouds of smoke. The din of battle was stunning, stupendous, deafening, as hundreds of the heaviest guns in the world gave tongue at once. All (officers) on board the Indefatigable, the Defence, and the Black Prince were lost; only four of the Queen Mary and two of the Invincible were saved. The list of (officers) killed numbers 333, and included Rear-Admirals Hood and Arbuthnot, whose flags were carried on the Invincible and Defence respectively.'

June 6 – 'H.M.S. Hampshire, with Lord Kitchener and his staff on board, was sunk last night about 8 p.m. to the west of Orkneys either by mine or torpedo … there is little hope of there being any survivors. H.M.S. Hampshire was on her way to Russia.'

1917

January 27 – 'A terrific north-easterly gale, which had raged from yesterday afternoon and was still raging with great fury in Start Bay this morning, appears to have played havoc with the little fishing village of Hallsands. Telephoning at 11.30 this morning from Torcross a correspondent says: 'The weather in Start Bay is terrific, and the scene one of awe and wonderment. Tremendous

seas are running in the bay, and already Hallsands has suffered badly; it is virtually wiped out, only two houses remaining of this old-world fishing hamlet.'

April 5 – 'The U.S. Senate has passed the resolution declaring a state of war with Germany by 82 votes to 6 at 11.15 p.m. after thirteen hours continuous debate. There was no demonstration when the result was announced.'

At the Cinedrome, Ebrington Street, Plymouth, Pearl White was starring in 'Annabel's Romance – a magnificent five-reel Pathe Colour Drama': at the Electric Theatre in Devonport, Olga Petrova, the peerless Russian emotional star appeared in an enthralling 'Metro' play entitled, 'Playing With Fire' – a photo-play of exceptional power, giving scope for a wonderful display of histrionic ability by the most beautiful of all Kinema stars.'

June 27 – 'The Committee on production and Distribution of Milk, of which Major the Hon Waldorf Astor, M.P., is chairman, expressed the opinion that the total consumption of milk might in the interests of children be considerably increased.'

1918

October 26 – 'The large and representative gathering at the funeral of Dame Agnes Weston, which took place this morning at the Corporation Cemetery, Weston Mill, showed how deep and general was the respect in which the deceased was held. It was a Naval funeral, and a vast concourse of people assembled. The funeral party left the Royal Sailors' Rest at 10.45, the coffin being carried on a gun-carriage and covered with the Union Jack. After 45 years of strenuous labour to the Glory of God and the good of the Service, Dame Weston rested from her labours. The earth was poorer and heaven the richer because the Sailors's Friend had passed away.'

October 27 – 'We are informed that some

boy vendors of *Evening Heralds* at Devonport yesterday charged twopence for the paper. 'No one should pay more than the published price, namely, one penny.'

November 11 – 'News of the signing of the armistice reached us this morning before nine o'clock through the courtesy of the Admiralty Headquarters at Mount Wise. A veritable pandemonium arose in the Dockyard and district: scores of sirens rent the air with their shrill blasts and big steamer horns boomed out their deep-throated message. At last the world war had come to an end. School children demonstrated to their hearts' content, marching along the principal streets singing and cheering and exchanging greetings on all sides. One procession had as leader the ubiquitous Charlie Chaplin replete with moustache, cane and preposterous boots.'

1919

May 31 – 'The American aeroplane N.C.4. left Ferrol, North-West Spain, just before 6.30 this morning, and, flying magnificently, reached Plymouth just before half-past two this afternoon in the closing stage of her transatlantic trip. The waiting crowds on the Hoe heard the hum of engines and presently the great seaplane appeared, followed by two British, and after circling the Sound descended gracefully amid the welcome of the shipping and the crowds.'

October 21 – 'Levant Mine, in West Cornwall, was the scene of a disastrous mining accident yesterday. It is feared that many lives were lost. At about 3 p.m. the rod of the 'man engine', a primitive arrangement used for raising and lowering the workers to and from various levels, broke at the nose at a moment when the engine was at the top of its stroke. The giant lift-ladder on which were probably over 100 men dropped 12-feet, causing great havoc.'

October 21 – 'A scheme for catching rats instituted in the naval establishments and ships at Devonport yesterday was given an incentive by the reward of 3d for every rat caught.'

December 2 – 'There came a hush at five and twenty minutes to four, a moment ever to be remembered in the history of the sex, when the folding-doors swung open, and Lady Astor stepped within the sacred Chamber. She was wearing a toque. So the great hat question has been settled by the lady herself.'

1920

February 12 – 'A proposal that the site (for a Plymouth War Memorial) should be Devonport Park was rejected despite the solidarity of a little bench of Devonport men who sat together. Other sites were referred to, including an unorthodox suggestion that Derry's Clock should be transferred elsewhere and give place to the new Memorial.'

House prices included such offers as: Vacant Possession – 15 miles Plymouth, delightful Freehold Residence comprising 2 reception, 6 bedrooms, fitted bathroom and offices, electric light, large garden, tennis court, near trains, golf, fishing, hunting. £1,600. For £750 there was a well-built, six-roomed house at Peverell, or, for the same price, a seven-roomed house at Mount Gould-road. A new Hillman 2-seater car with double 'Dickey' seat, painted blue, exceptionally smart, cost £590. New motor-cycles (on sale were such models as a $3\frac{1}{2}$hp Sunbeam; a $2\frac{1}{2}$hp Triumph or a 6hp Williamson Combination) from 175 guineas upwards.

October 4 – The French sailing vessel Yvonne struck the Breakwater and instantly the heavy seas drove it broadside on the structure. They launched the port boat. It was quickly damaged. Eventually they were all picked up, with the exception of the cook, Campbell, a coloured man of Jamaica. Commander Freyberg, the King's Harbourmaster, got into the water and went on the Breakwater to try and find him. It was a brave and gallant act, but he could not be found.'

1921

April 2 – 'Mr Charles Job, a Plymothian, who has interested himself in the question of the discharge of ex-Service men from Devonport Dockyard, addressed a letter on the subject to Lady Astor, M.P., in which he pointed out that there were many workers still employed in the Yard who possessed pensions or who had a certain amount of income accruing to them from other sources. The writer suggested that 'it would not cause much distress if they were the first to be discharged.'

April 23 – 'Yesterday was the 26th anniversary of the '*Herald*' which rushed into the ken of a surprised and startled world with all the suddenness of a Pons-Winnecke comet on a Monday morning in the Spring of 1895. It has since then extended its orbit considerably, but it completes the circuit every twenty-four hours with the utmost regularity.'

April 7 – 'Mr F.H. Pearse, of Plymouth, has contrived a vehicle which consists of a motor-car deprived of its engine and a bicycle, by means of which he supplies the driving power. His desire is to challenge the powers that be with a motor upon which he cannot be taxed. The car was the first private car to be seen in Plymouth. A $4^{1}/_{2}$hp Bens machine, it was built at Mannheim, Germany, and Mr Pearse bought it in 1901 for £240. Mr Pearse recalled the furore that the appearance of the car created on its appearance in Plymouth in 1901. Fear was the chief emotion provoked, and its driver knocked down a man in Union-street, and ran over his leg – which, fortunately, was a wooden one!'

THE HEARTS of the former Three Towns. Above, the slim, Italianate tower of Devonport market, built in 1852, lies buried behind the grim Dockyard Wall; right, Derry's Cross Clocktower (1863), Plymouth, is eclipsed by the Theatre Royal.

THE THIRD vital centre was the elegant Stonehouse Town Hall (1850), a blitz casualty whose shell was hastily demolished in August 1946.

August 14 – A Napoleon of the Press: 'The whole Empire will receive with regret the news that Viscount Northcliffe's illness terminated fatally soon after ten o'clock this morning. He leaves no heir, and his title becomes extinct. His six brothers include Lord Rothermere, Sir Leicester Harmsworth M.P., Mr Cecil Harmsworth, M.P., and Mr Hildebrand Harmsworth. If Northcliffe lowered the standard of journalism, he raised the status of the journalist. He made journalism a career for all the talents.'

August 19 – 'Mrs Patrick Campbell will appear at the Royal Theatre next week in the great American success, 'Voodoo', and Mrs Campbell will be supported by her London company augmented by a number of negro actors and singers specially brought from America. Notable among them is Mr Paul Robeson, the champion athlete of America.'

November 16 – 'The prompt publication of election results in the windows of 'the *Western Morning News and Mercury*' attracted a large crowd, which from 11 o'clock

onwards grew to such an extent that the street was densely packed for many yards.'

November 24 – 'The Committee of the Mayor's Unemployment Fund this morning considered the problem of relieving the unemployed during the winter. The fund now totals only £459, and £50 is being spent weekly. At the present time the fund was relieving 324 cases, a total that involved 1,271 dependants … they were getting many demands for boots and coal where sickness was prevailing.'

1923

May 31 – Jutland Day: 'It is a bitter thing that so soon we should forget the long-drawn battle between grey shapes on a grey sea, which made England safe and bottled the floating fortresses of Germany within her harbours, and, in the end spelt check-mate to the would-be War Lords of the world. Seven thousand Britons laid down their lives on that day for you and me in that victory you and I and the almanac forgot – seven thousand men from the Westcountry and from the North and from those ancient Sussex sea-towns … My masters, it is an evil thing that we should forget so soon so great a day.'

September 17 – 'The municipal and mercantile authorities in Plymouth have, along with the De Havilland Air Service amply demonstrated the Plymouth-Manchester-Belfast air passenger and mail service, and it is expected that when General Brancker visits Plymouth early next month it will be announced that the service will be permanent. The D.H. 50 'Galatea' arrived back from Manchester at 2.40 p.m. today at Roborough, after an epic struggle against the fury of the storms.'

September – 'While Crownhill may view with delight the prospects held out by advocates of amalgamation with Plymouth, a representative of this paper was unable to find any symptoms of joy in Torpoint in regard to the suggestion that the Tamarside community

would be willing to co-operate in the formation of a yet greater Plymouth.'

1924

April 1 – 'I declare this road free to the public for ever.' These were the simple words uttered by the Mayor of Plymouth today at each of the five toll-gates which for so long have hampered the traffic of the great highways of the borough. The biggest crowd was assembled on Stonehouse Bridge. The Mayor delivered a short address before severing the tape: 'We rejoice that we have lived to see the day when the union of the Three Towns is an accomplished fact. We hold out the hand of fellowship to those who live in the western part of the borough.'

July 29 – 'Prince George today unveiled the Navy War Memorial on Plymouth Hoe in the presence of a vast assembly (estimated at 25,000). The Last Post, the grandest of all service calls, came from an unexpected quarter, the top of the old Smeaton lighthouse. The poignant notes of the silver bugles of the Marines went searching, ever-searching, through the morning air until it seemed as though they must echo over every sea grave of those who had paid the supreme sacrifice.'

July 30 – 'A good deal of banter arising out of the proposed application of Plympton District Council for urban powers was exchanged between Plymouth and Plympton guests following the official opening by Prince George of the tuberculosis colony at Efford yesterday. Mr Priest said it was up to each authority to have a vision for the future, and when they had the proper feeling of mutual co-operation it would be the better for both.'

1925

The BBC had begun broadcasting at Plymouth: the *Herald* advertised the programmes (Call 5PY 338m). On offer were such 'Afternoon topic' temptations as

'Wobert Blow my Powwidge' by Miss Margot Hirons, or the intriguing 'Farmer Stubbs Attends Church Parade.' Of special interest, however, was the debut of the 2LO String Orchestra on July 19. Programmes began at 3.30 p.m. and closed down with a performance of the Savoy Bands at midnight.

June – 'Beef (per lb) – sirloin, undercut, wing cut, from 1s 6d to 1s 8d; ribs 1s 2d to 1s 4d; rump steak with bone 1s 6d to 1s 8d, boneless 1s 8d to 1s 10d; topside 1s 4d to 1s 6d; brisket 9d to 10d; Mutton – Legs 1s 4d to 1s 6d; breast 8d to 10d; shoulder 1s to 1s 2d. Pork – legs 1s 1d to 1s 2d; shoulder 10d to 1s; bacon 1s to 1s 4d; heads 3d to 4d.'

July 21 – 'That it was hoped to return to the penny postage within the lifetime of the present Parliament was the statement made by the Postmaster-General in the House of Commons yesterday.'

August 3 – 'Fines were imposed at Liskeard on the drivers of three 29-seater charabancs belonging to the Plymouth Co-operative Society for driving between Bodmin and Liskeard on June 30 at a speed exceeding 12 miles per hour, contrary to the Heavy Motor Order, 1904. Supt. J.H. Drew stated that on June 30 a constable at Bodmin called up a constable at Liskeard on the telephone, and after they had compared watches a message was received at Liskeard that the first defendant had left at a certain time. He was stopped at Liskeard and informed he had exceeded the speed limit between the two towns having travelled the 13 miles in 47 minutes, at a rate of over 16 miles an hour. The defendant gave evidence in which he admitted exceeding 18 miles in an hour.'

'No 7 Maple-grove, Mutley, an attractive residence of 9 rooms was offered with vacant possession, but withdrawn at £1,090. No 30 Tracy-street, Plymouth, a seven-roomed house, vacant possession of five of the rooms being offered, was sold for £610.'

July 25 – 'Devonport Market – Potatoes 10d to 1s 2d per stone; parsnips 2d, carrots 1½d, onions 1½d per lb; cauliflower 2d to 4d each; tomatoes 5d to 8d per lb; grapes 6d per lb; coconuts 4d each; chestnuts 4p per lb; bananas 1½d each; butter 2s 2d per lb; eggs 3/- a dozen; rabbits 1s 1d each; cream 2s 4d per lb.' 'The year 1924 was the wettest year in Great Britain since 1903, according to a Stationery Office publication just issued.'

November 27 – 'Amid the rich pageantry of State ceremonial and the simple homage of the people, the remains of Queen Alexandra were reverently borne to Westminster Abbey, where a great and solemn service was held prior to their interment among the Royal tombs of historic Windsor. There were four Kings in the cortege. Before dawn people began to congregate along the route to take a farewell of the beloved Queen-Mother. They were mostly poor, humble folk … snow fell heavily during the morning.'

1926

May 4 – Nation in Grip of General Strike: 'Plymouth's intention of rallying to meet the national emergency was demonstrated by the fact that in the first hour of recruiting in the Guildhall 400 enrolled. Electricians, motor mechanics, doctors, tram drivers and owner-drivers of cars were among the volunteers. Men are recruited under this scheme in the interests of the community, and not for the purpose of acting as strike breakers.'

May 6 – *Morning News* and *Evening Herald* and the Strike: 'Despite the existence of a National Agreement, under which a fortnight's notice must be given before declaring a strike or lock-out, our workmen yesterday went on strike without giving any notice at all. The *Western Evening Herald* repudiates connection with the typescript sheet published in Plymouth yesterday.

May 7 – 'Members of the staff of the *Western Evening Herald*, with one or two exceptions, returned to duty yesterday afternoon.'

May 8 – 'The partial resumption of the

Plymouth tramway service this morning was marked by disorderly scenes in Old Town-street towards midday, when the police drew their batons. Very large crowds lined the thoroughfare, and during one outburst of hostility, as a tramcar and an omnibus were passing, a man and a woman were arrested. Several times it was found necessary for police officers to mount the footboards and assist in piloting the tramcars through the angry masses. The excitement was very evident amongst the women, some of whom went so far as to clamber on to the front of cars whilst they were in motion and spit in the face of the drivers.'

SPECIAL SUNDAY STRIKE EDITION: **May 9** – 'Scenes of violent disorder broke the hitherto peaceful course of the strike at Plymouth yesterday afternoon, and several persons were arrested. Angry crowds of strikers gathered in Old Town-street and Drake-circus, attacks being made on the (tram)cars at mid-day and later in the afternoon, when a vast multitude of people congested the thoroughfare. At six, the cars were withdrawn. Mounted police cleared the main avenue from Drake-circus to Spooners Corner.'

May 10 – 'Unique indeed was the football match at Home Park. The famous enclosure was the scene of a game between teams representing the strikers and the Plymouth Police. After preliminary handshakes had been exchanged, the Chief Constables's wife kicked off. The strikers won by two goals to one.'

May 12 – 'When the news came through that the general strike had been called off, many refused to believe it had collapsed so suddenly; at Dockers' Hall and Sutton Labour Party offices in Treville-street, it was received with shouts of Lies and Rot.'

In **August**, the list of British submarine disasters was augmented by the accidental sinking of Submarine H29 in the dockyard while undergoing refit. The accident, which was attended by the death of one naval rating and five civilian workmen occurred with dramatic suddenness, many other workers narrowly escaping death as the cascades of water poured through the conning hatches.

1927

January 4 – 'Len Harvey of Plymouth was badly beaten in a twenty rounds contest on points at the Ring, London, last night by Len Johnson, the coloured middle-weight from Manchester.'

March 1 – 'Two hundred people are living at Ernesettle Camp, St Budeaux, in 12-year-old Army huts, which are rotting over their heads. Driven to seek temporary accommodation at the camp by the acute housing shortage, which Plymouth experienced after the war, they have been there ever since. Now they are under notice to quit and have nowhere to go.'

March 4 – 'Over 200 miles of roads and lanes receive attention from an army of workers every week … visitors frequently comment upon the cleanliness of Plymouth's highways. Plymouth ranks among the cleanest towns in the country.'

March – 'Mr H.H. Saunders has just completed ten years in the Office of Chief Constable of Plymouth. The authorised strength of the Plymouth force is 266, and the local fire brigade is composed of members of the force. In 1917 there were 563 licenced houses in Plymouth, the number had been reduced to 497.'

March 14 – 'The trading community and the economists on the Town Council are not sharing the enthusiasm of the educationists that Plymouth is to be the first town to have a by-law raising the school-leaving age from 14 to 15 years.'

1928

June 1 – 'After her quickest trip for the year, the French liner France arrived at Plymouth this morning with 697 passengers. She will be followed to Plymouth tomorrow by the Carmania and the Lapland … the Plymouth Chamber of Commerce has concluded that Plymouth's geographical position so far as the sea is concerned makes it pre-eminent as a port of call. Both passengers and mail can be, and are, landed with speed and a minimum of expense.

July – 'The Clyno Engineering Company (1920) Ltd., Wolverhampton, will market a new nine horse-power car at a price just over £100. This follows the announcement that Morris Motors are preparing a seven horse-power model: the price of the 'baby' Austin is £135. That of the new small Morris has not yet been fixed.'

July – 'A table showing the number of persons per mile in each county in England and Wales has been circulated in Hansard by the Ministry of Transport. Devon: mileage of all roads on March 31, 1927, 7,770, population 440,023, number of persons per mile 57. Cornwall: mileage of roads 4,391, population 320,559, persons per mile 73. Somerset; mileage of roads 4,675, population 397,034, persons per mile 85.'

October 17 – 'It was officially notified to the Mayor of Plymouth to-day that the King had been pleased to decree the raising of the town to the status of a city. The intimation added that His Majesty's action had been taken on the recommendation of the Home Secretary.'

PLYMOUTH ARGYLE—1929-30

Back Row:— M. Russell, H. Bland, N. Mackay, F. Craig, F. McKenzie, F. Titmuss, A. Hardie, T. Haynes (Trainer).
Front Row:— A. Matthews, T. Grozier, F. Sloan, J. Vidler, R. Bowden, J. Leslie, S. Black.
Inset Left:— H. Cann.
Inset Right:— J. Pullen

PLYMOUTH Argyle 1929-1930, including the legendary duo Jack Leslie and Sammy Black.

31

1929

October 14 – 'The outbreak of typhoid fever at Polperro was traced to the general absence of sanitary facilities: the consequent pollution of the river which flows through the village renders the water from the stream totally unfit for domestic purposes, however remotely connected with the preparation of food or drink for human consumption.' (Ministry of Health report).

October 14 – 'I am opposed to imported labour in this county. I think it will create difficulties in days to come,' said Mr Isaac Foot, M.P., addressing the Liberal Association at Liskeard.'

October 21 – 'One cannot get a decent meal in Plymouth, there is nowhere to dance, and you can do with some more kinemas. A few Americans would soon brighten up the place. Plymouth people do not realise the money there is to be made if they would do more to attract people to the city.' (Actress, Miss Joy Ashley).

October 17 – 'Intense public interest is being manifested, throughout the country, in the Drake election petition in the names of Messrs N.J.P. Revington and A.T. Easterbrook against the return of Mr James John Hamlyn Moses as Parliamentary representative of the Drake Division … **October 25** – 'Amid great tension, after a hearing lasting eight days, Mr Justice Swift this afternoon pronounced judgement to the effect that the Drake Division election petition must be dismissed … The *Western Evening Herald* commented: 'It is no exaggeration to say that the City of Plymouth as a whole shared in a sigh of relief … local Labour folk were bitterly angry that a petition should be lodged against Plymouth's first Labour M.P. Universal comment has been made upon the inconspicuousness of the two gentlemen whose names figure as the petitioners. Their part seems to have ended with the signing of the petition, for they were not called into the witness-box … Perhaps when the historians get to work in years to come they will be able to reveal who were the persons behind the petition …'

October 22 – 'Len Harvey, the Plymouth boxer, last night retained the title of middle-weight champion of Great Britain by beating Jack Hood, the Birmingham challenger, on points in a fifteen- round contest, which went the full distance, at the Stadium, London. Harvey (who weighed in at 11st 2lb) was a popular winner, if applause counted for anything … '

October 23 – 'The charges made against the Conservatives and Liberals of deliberately neglecting the interests of the city was an attempt to misrepresent and delude the electors. Mr Lovell R. Dunstan mentioned in disproof (of the charges) the Embankment- road scheme, the Hyde Park-corner improvement, the construction of Swilly-road, and the huge sum spent on housing, the acquisition of the Central Park, on education and public health. Since the armistice the city had spent over one and a quarter millions in providing work for the unemployed … he denied that the Council were asking the Government to permit a new valuation of the city to be made.'

1930

April 2 – 'There were nearly 5,000 fewer clergymen in the Church of England in 1928 than in 1921, and if the present rate of decrease was maintained they would be an extinct species in England and Wales in 30 years. Mr. C.E.M. Joad complained clergymen were absorbed in controversies over technical matters of no interest to the layman.'

September – 'The Deliverer' for August is essentially a Plymouth number, dealing as it does almost entirely with the Salvation Army women's social work in the city. No 2, The Octagon, the first address of social work in Plymouth, was opened in 1889. A few years later premises were built in King-street and opened as a hostel for women. Writing of her work in King-street, the warden, Miss Soper said: 'We long to make a mark upon the wicked neighbourhood around us. Yesterday one poor, drunken woman came to our door asking us to buy her baby for twopence! Poor, unwanted, unloved little ones – what a pity the Salvation Army cannot gather them all in.' A maid, on hearing the Army was coming to take in washing at Mannamead, exclaimed in horror: 'The slums are coming!' to which a 'Trophy of Grace' replied with dignity: 'We are not slum, we are social.' Lieut-Col Soper (retired) is a sister of Mrs Bramwell Booth, and was the first who sat in the Plymouth Police Courts and to whom the magistrates began handing over the refractory girls. Adjutant Drury is asking for a million farthings. A farthing is only a very little thing, yet it bears the King's head and so it has worth and value. She wants them to clear the two Plymouth homes of debt.'

August 30 – 'The fact that the visit of Miss Amy Johnson to the city takes place during Plymouth Week is a happy coincidence. She will arrive at Roborough on Wednesday afternoon, September 24. It remains only for the public to see to it that she is greeted in a manner which the intrepid flyer deserves.'

August 21 – 'It is feared that several lives have been lost in the wreck of the yacht Islander in Lansallos Bay, between Fowey and Polruan. Coastguards descended the cliff face and threw a line over the vessel, but it was not held. The Islander, a yacht of about 31 tons, drifted off after first stranding, but was subsequently thrown back again in the stormy weather which prevailed. That there were women on board the unfortunate craft is assured, for their voices and screams were heard above the storm ... **August 22** – 'It has now been established that six lives were lost in the disaster. The body of a man washed up at Lansallos Bay this morning was found to be that of Commodore H.D. King, the Unionist M.P. for South Paddington. A second body was brought into Looe this afternoon, having been found by a mackerel boat ...

August 23 – 'Sir Arthur Quiller-Couch, the famous author, of Fowey, said that the watching service had been cut down to 850 for the whole coast of 4,000 miles, and that seemed totally inadequate. The great coastguard service has been jettisoned.'

1931

January – 'The past year (1930) cannot be looked back upon in Cornwall with any degree of pleasure whatever. The last returns showed that there were 8,793 on the books of the Employment Exchanges, as compared with 4,413 for the corresponding period of 1929. In the previous great depression in tin mining in 1922 there were 5,064 unemployed.'

January 2 – The Dole Enquiry: 'Abuses (of the dole system) are so flagrant as to provide cause for wonder that even the Socialist Government should allow them to go on. A system which, if it does not actually incite men and women to dishonesty, has created a condition of affairs under which the public purse is regarded as a fair mark for plunder …'

January 7 – 'Ships of the Atlantic Fleet based on Devonport came down to harbour preparatory to leaving for the spring cruise tomorrow. The cruiser Dorsetshire and the minesweeper Adventure were already in the Sound, and the first to join them this morning was the Renown, one of the most beautiful ships in the British Navy. The Rodney has been in the Sound since last Friday. The ships presented an extraordinarily fine spectacle as they lay at anchor on a dazzling sea.'

February 5 – 'Divers and drifters were this morning making every effort to salvage that part of the ill-fated flying boat (a Blackburn Iris) which crashed in Plymouth Sound yesterday and still remains in deep water with presumably the bodies of the (nine) men who are missing.'

1932

On **Sunday, January 24,** the *Herald* broke the Sabbath quiet. The cause was electrifying: a full-scale riot at one of the world's most famous gaols, Dartmoor Prison. A seven-column wide banner headline proclaimed: Sensational Mutiny at Princetown. 'The main buildings of Princetown Prison are now blazing furiously. This is but one of the phases of the most serious affair which has ever occurred in the long history of Dartmoor Prison since the slaughter of the American prisoners at Princetown over 100 years ago. Shortly after nine o'clock this morning, a large body of the prisoners, amongst whom discontent had been seething for a week, broke out into open mutiny when the convicts assembled for church parade. Policemen were rushed to the scene from Exeter and Plymouth and, after twenty minutes' truncheon battle, succeeded in subduing them. Ominous rumours soon spread outside the prison, and the utmost excitement speedily manifested among the residents. Convicts had got hold of some musical instruments from the chapel, and one was playing bugle calls. A great number remained loyal. There were in the prison altogether 480: 200 to 300 are estimated to have taken part in the riot. Between 130 and 150 prison officials were on duty. Plymouth Fire Brigade were sent for and got to work speedily. The centre block and tower and clock are destroyed.'

January 25 – 'The great Cup-tie between Arsenal and Plymouth Argyle is over, and the shouts of the vast multitude of 65,311 who packed Highbury for the attractive fourth round struggle have faded into the background. Argyle lost by 4 goals to 2.'

1933

January – 'Unemployment, the greatest social problem of the age, has had the greatest claim on the time of the Royal Family during 1932. Led by the Prince of Wales, they devoted unsparing time and attention to the welfare of the 'out-of-works.' Four times the Prince has made tours to investigate conditions of the unemployed and to spread by his own example his doctrine of help for others. In his own Duchy of Cornwall, the Prince has talked to the unfortunates and to those who are helping them.'

January 6 – 'With a roar of engines and clanging bells the fire engine and escape dash through the street of Plymouth, and in their train follows the ever-vigilant, ever-ready St John Ambulance. When next you see this sight remember that inside the ambulance rests a wonderful invention – a machine which may restore human life when seemingly all is lost. Suffocation, drowning, gas poisoning – this machine combats their effects so readily that sixty per cent of the cases in which it is utilized has been successful. The Plymouth Central Ambulance Station was one of the first in the country at which the new apparatus – the Novox Resuscitation apparatus, as it is called – was installed.'

January 12 – 'Accommodation more adequate to their needs would be provided by the conversion of the old prison building at Mutley, Plymouth, into a central police station, magistrates' court, childrens' and coroner's court, weights and measures office, probation office, fire station and mortuary.'

January 13 – 'Efforts to salvage the R.A.F. Iris flying boat which crashed into a naval Dockyard launch in Plymouth Sound were continued today, but were hampered by fog. It now seems certain that one man lost his life in the mishap, and the search for the missing aircraftsman, who is a Plymothian, continues. The attitude of the Mount Batten authorities throughout has been in striking contrast to that adopted by those in authority at the station two years ago, when the disaster in which nine lives were lost occurred. It may have been technically accurate to say that the 'mishap did not concern the public' but the public of Plymouth take a deep interest in the activities of the R.A.F. at Mount Batten, and might, therefore, have been worthy of some consideration. It was stated on the Plymouth Barbican today that when the last fatality occurred several local fishermen offered to trawl the Sound for the missing men. The heavy trawl nets sink to the bottom of the sea, and it is contended in this fashion bodies would be found within a comparatively short time. The men offered their services free of charge.'

January 29 – 'The annual report of the Medical Officer of Health revealed the general sanitary arrangements in some of the elementary schools of Plymouth leave much to be desired.'

January 30 – Herr Hitler as New Chancellor of Germany: 'There was a surprise development in the political situation in Germany today when it was announced that Adolf Hitler, the Nazi chief, has been appointed Chancellor.'

1934

July 10 – 'The sword of Drake, believed to be the only one in existence, is to return to Plymouth. Efforts are to be made for the weapon to be on view during Navy Week in the city. For many years the sword has been in a glass case in the officers' mess at Portsmouth Barracks, but when the name of the barracks at Devonport was changed from Vivid to Drake, steps were taken in an endeavour to transfer it to Devonport. It is a family heirloom of Mr Godfrey H Williams of St Lawrence, Jersey.'

July 10 – 'The Chief Constable of Cornwall, who applied for the provision of telephones in five police houses, said there were 77 police houses in the county with telephones, and 60 without.'

September 14 – Letters to The Editor: 'Sir, If only those women and girls who plaster their lips with red rouge knew what frights they looked I am sure many of them would give up the practice. In a few years to come I should not be surprised if women took to wearing horns on their foreheads and rings in their noses just to complete their barbaric appearance. Son of Devon, Plymouth.'

September 19 – 'Devonport Mercantile Association agreed to meet Plymouth Chamber of Commerce to discuss ways and means of proceeding with the Tamar Tunnel scheme. The tunnel would cost in the neighbourhood of £1,211,000. Mr W Roseveare, civil engineer, explained his latest proposal was to construct a tunnel starting at the junction of Catherine-street and Market-street (Devonport), making a slight curve to immediately under 76 Fore- street, next to the Royal Hotel, and thence in a straight line to Gravesend Point, Torpoint. The scheme would consist of 100-feet of cutting at the Devonport end, 4,687-feet of tunnel and 900-feet of open channel cutting at the Torpoint end, the gradients at either end being one in 20, and under the river section, one in 23. Mr Roseveare proposed that the internal diameter of the tunnel should be 27ft 6ins, which permitted a 19ft roadway and one 4ft 6ins raised footpath.'

September 19 – 'Plymouth is the only place in the West Country included in the 36 areas 'chiefly responsible for the continuance of an exceptionally high maternal mortality rate for a long period.' The rate for Plymouth has been 5.44 whereas the figure for the whole country has been 4.32.'

September 6 – 'Mr Hore-Belisha (Transport Minister and M.P. for Devonport) has made yet another good move in the campaign for reducing the terrible toll of death and injury on the roads. He has decided to set up a Standing Road Safety Council. Hitherto, motorists have fumed about the wicked three-abreast cyclists, the cyclists have raged furiously over the arrogant motorists, and pedestrians have called a plague upon you both.'

September 6 – 'Sir Frederick Winnicott was unable to be present at the interesting ceremony which marked the presentation

PRE-WAR Basket-street (left), Bedford-street, and one of Devonport MP Leslie Hore-Belisha's pedestrian crossings in the foreground.

yesterday of the Mayflower memorial he has given to the city. It was appropriate that the ceremony should be devoid of ostentatious splendour, for that would not have been in keeping with the spirit of the Pilgrim Fathers.'

1935

May 18 – 'Plymouth Guildhall last night was the scene of an historic assembly – a banquet to celebrate the bestowal of the honour of the Lord Mayoralty upon the city. It was a brilliant spectacle expressing the municipality's delight at the occasion ... Lady Astor M.P. said they should remember that it was a Jubilee gift ... they might have failed without the definite and active help of the Prince of Wales (Lord High Steward of Plymouth) for his very deep interest in the city of Plymouth.'

May 21 – 'Accidental Death, was the ver-

dict at the inquest today on Lawrence of Arabia (Mr Thomas Edward Shaw) at the Wool Military Hospital, Bovington Camp, Dorset, where for six days a desperate fight was made to save his life. Lawrence was fatally injured on Monday of last week in a collision between his motor-cycle and a boy cyclist.'

May 31 – 'Tomorrow, the former Government House at Mount Wise will change its name to Admiralty House, and will in future be the new offices of the Commander-in-Chief. It has been repaired and altered at a cost of £4,650. The original Admiralty House is to be transferred to the Army authorities.'

May 2 – 'There are now at Devonport three of the six aircraft carriers in the Royal Navy. They are the Furious, of the Home Fleet, and the Glorious and Eagle of the Mediterranean Fleet. Total expenditure on refit of the Glorious is estimated at £435,846.

which includes £167,000 for Dockyard labour.'

1936

January 28 – 'Plymouth's day of national mourning (for King George V) started with the firing of seventy minute guns from the naval saluting battery at Eastern King's: the Army took up the salute from the ramparts of the Royal Citadel.'

March 21 – 'An increase in crime in Plymouth during last year is revealed in the report of the Chief Constable (Mr W.O. Johnson). The total number of indictable offences was 1,433, the second highest figure since 1926. This table shows the growth of crime: 1926, 616; 1927, 741; 1928, 780; 1929, 832; 1930, 898; 1931, 961; 1932, 1,580; 1933, 1,350; 1934, 1,423; 1935, 1,433.'

August 23 – 'There was a most unusual occurrence at Plymouth last night, thousands of pilchards coming right into Sutton Pool and being easily taken in nets in three or four feet of water. During the siege of Plymouth in 1643 the starving inhabitants were saved by a similar visitation.'

December 5 – 'Work on the North-road station extensions at Plymouth has begun. The first job in hand is the widening of the bridge over Pennycomequick-hill. It will, when completed, carry four lines, and double the width of the present structure.'

December 11 – 'Parliament proceeded with the stately courtesy of mediaeval times with the business of passing the Abdication Bill. King Edward VIII awaited in the quiet seclusion of Fort Belvedere the news of the passing of the Act which ends his short reign.'

1937

March 15 – 'With seaplanes hovering overhead, motor boats and sailing craft dashing to and fro, eager throngs crowding the slopes of the Hoe, the Queen Mary, pride of the British Merchant Navy, holder of the Blue Riband of the Atlantic, proud flagship of the Cunard White Star, was welcomed to Plymouth today, when she made the first of a series of four calls, arriving from New York at 11 a.m.

A FEW years later the scene had been blasted from existence: the spire of the ruined Charles Church rises left.

The slopes of the Hoe were thronged with spectators long before the great ship hove into sight.'

May 12 – 'The heart of Plymouth throbbed out its loyalty in a stirring scene on that most historic of all venues, the Hoe. A vast concourse, estimated at between 50,000 and 60,000 people, made the background to their testimony of allegiance and general acclamation of the new King and Queen a united religious service. On this great and memorable scene the sun shone. Then from the north came a vivid flash of lightning, illuminating the dull skies, and over the city there rumbled the thunder.'

May 28 – 'It was in 1874 that the first telephone to be installed in England was set up and operated at Torr (home of the Bayly family, later tenanted by the Devonport Blind Institution) on the occasion of a visit to Plymouth from America of Mr Graham Bell, who came to exhibit his invention and lecture to the British Association which assembled at the town that year.'

December 1937 – 'A village of about 4,000 people is springing up at Efford, Plymouth, where farms and fields previously existed.' ·

1938

May 2 – 'Screen star Marlene Dietrich was among the passengers in the Queen Mary when the crack British liner arrived at Plymouth today. She had not completed dressing when newspaper photographers called at her cabin this morning. The star was in a charming mood. With 447 cabin, 444 tourist and 483 third class passengers, the Queen Mary, flagship of the Cunard White Star fleet, had arrived off Penlee Point at 9.50 a.m. after a voyage of 4 days 9 hours 6 minutes from New York.'

May 28 – 'To the roar of high-powered aero engines and the thrilled murmur of the crowd, Empire Air Day at Roborough Airport today was an exciting success. The highlight was undoubtedly the high-speed individual aerobatics given by a Hawker Fury interceptor fighter of 43 Squadron, Tangmere. At times the Fury touched 300 miles an hour in power dives. The repertoire included upward, rocket and slow rolls, and a roll off the top of the loop.'

May 9 – 'Lord Astor writes: The fiction that has been written recently about an imaginary group described as the 'Cliveden Set' was better ignored … but now it has figured in debates of the House of Commons. For years my wife and I have entertained in the country members of all parties (including Communists). To link our week-ends with any particular clique is as absurd as is the allegation that those of us who desire to establish better relations with Germany or with Italy are pro-Nazis or pro-Fascists. Lady Astor and I are no more Fascists today than we were Communists a few years ago … '

1939

May 6 – 'One of Plymouth's finest residences has been purchased by the British Broadcasting Corporation for new studios, concert hall, and office accommodation for the city. Ingledene, Seymour-road, Mannamead – one-time residence of the famous Sir James Douglass, builder of one of the Eddystone lighthouses.'

May 6 – 'All kinds of plans for improving the pay – at present fixed at a shilling a day – and the conditions of the 200,000 twenty-years-old Militia-men who will be called up this year for compulsory training are to be brought forward next week in the Commons.'

September 1 – 'During today and the two coming days approximately 20,000 child evacuees will be arriving in Devon, and 4,800 women and children in Cornwall. The eventual total in the second county is to be about 34,350.'

Sunday, September 3 – 'Britain is now at war with Germany. The Prime Minister made this fateful announcement to the nation today in the absence of any reply to the British and French ultimatum which expired at 11 a.m. Rumours and hopes of a last-minute peace through Italian intervention had proved false. At 11.30 a.m. came the dramatic flash to the *Herald* offices: 'Raid warning on London. Creed (news receiving apparatus) closing down.'

1940

February 15 – 'Battle-scarred still, H.M.S. Exeter sailed into Plymouth Sound today with over 500 men of the Westcountry aboard, safe home after bearing the greatest sea fight of this war. As when H.M.S. Ajax reached Plymouth, thousands of citizens lined the waterfront to welcome their heroes. This time the welcome was more fervent and more tragic. The men aboard this ship were from Plymouth and the Westcountry. Many in the waterfront crowds had husbands, sons or brothers aboard. And some could not cheer. Sixty men of this ship's company sleep for ever beneath South Atlantic waves, victims of the Graf Spee's guns. Not only did Plymouth honour this ship. At Mount Wise Mr Winston Churchill, First Lord of the Admiralty, took the salute as Exeter steamed up the Hamoaze … every ship in the Sound greeted proud H.M.S. Exeter with siren hoots and cheers for the crew. Her flags were flying, her decks lined with ratings, her Marine band playing on her quarter-deck.'

June 4 – 'Despite continual attacks from the air and by long-range artillery, troops are still embarking from Dunkirk in large numbers.'

September 16 – 'The man who saved St Paul's Cathedral from the giant one-ton time-bomb which threatened to level the great Wren structure has had his home in Plymouth for the past twelve years. He is Lieut. R. Davies, R.E. of Park-street. He was responsible for the extricating, removing and detonating of the bomb.'

1941

March 22 – 'Smouldering ruins, razed buildings, homeless people, men, women and children trapped beneath debris, many dead. This was the trail left by the Nazis after their second wanton attack on Plymouth last night, in which it is estimated that at least 20,000 incendiary bombs and hundreds of high explosives were showered on shopping and residential parts of the city. The attack was more severe than that of the previous night. When fires were burning the Huns continued their devilish work by dive bombing the blazing ruins. You could read a newspaper by the glow of the flames several miles away. Sharing Plymouth's ordeal was Mr G Menzies, Australian Prime Minister, who arrived in the town shortly before the attack began. He is known to be safe.'

March 27 – 'When the detailed story of Plymouth's raids can be told there will be no finer chapter than that telling how the hospitals, their doctors and nurses, worked on unperturbed amid buildings often ringed with fire and explosions. Dr T Peirson, Medical Officer of Health, told the *Herald* today that when one large hospital suffered direct hits, causing fatalities among patients and staff, the doctors and nurses dealt with their own casualties and carried on with the work of admitting and treating cases throughout the night.'

March 31 – 'How fire-watchers, some of them elderly women, performed exploits of heroism in saving valuable property belonging to the churches of St Andrew's and St Catherine's forms a chapter of gallantry which must be written of the two devastating raids on Plymouth. The mother church of Plymouth is now an empty shell, and thus the daughter church of St Catherine's, herself well over a century old, takes on the mantle. Fortunately St Catherine's is intact, its existence tremendously due to the magnificent work done by the curate in charge (Rev F.B. Yarker) and two school-teacher voluntary

WINSTON Churchill accompanied by his wife and Lady Astor, left, toured Plymouth in a larger Daimler in May 1941. The destruction grieved him deeply.

fire-watchers Miss B Bancroft and Miss Worder. Incendiaries fell through the roof, but were boldly tackled. Gradually the situation became too hot for these courageous fire-fighters. While the incumbent remained at the church the two women gathered the plate - the goblets, salvers, alms-dish - in their arms and fled in the direction of the Hoe. They saved the church plate.'

April 21 – 'Plymouth, with her wounds steadily healing from the blitz of the 20th and 21st of last month, suffered one of the new Nazi double blitzes last night - again the 21st of the month. Stories of heroism of A.R.P. personnel, police and members of the fighting Services will never be fully told - they were performed without thought of the consequences. Two churches and three kinemas were destroyed: incendiaries fell on a theatre: a mother who yesterday heard her son was missing stood before her ruined house when a telegram arrived saying her husband was dead.'

May 5 – 'Memories of the days of peace came flooding back to the sound of martial music on Plymouth Hoe yesterday. The Lord Mayor recently suggested to the military authorities that if a band were available it might give concerts on the Hoe. The response was immediate, and a band will be playing on the promenade from 4 to 5 today and other days at various times.'

1942

March 12 – 'Lord Woolton dropped a not unexpected bombshell yesterday when he announced that nothing white whether bread, buns, cakes or biscuits would be made on and from April 20. The manager of a Plymouth bakers told the *Herald* that he thought the new bread would not be so bad as in the last war.'

April 1 – 'A limited number of oranges have arrived in Plymouth and will be available in shops from tomorrow. The oranges will be issued at the rate of one pound per head to children.'

May 22 – 'Nearly 60,000 people applied for their ration books at Plymouth in the first four days.'

October 31 – 'Plymouth City Police, co-operating with the police of the three Services and National Service officials, carried out another round-up of war service dodgers last night when they paid a surprise visit to a fun-fair, where there was a crowd of about 400 people – mostly young Service men and young civilians. They had a sensational reception. As they entered and closed the main exit they were met with a choking, almost impenetrable smoke screen. Practically coincidental with their entry a soldier at the far end of the fair ground ignited a smoke bomb. There was a general stampede for the main exit many not knowing it was closed with the police barring the way. Despite these handicaps, the police and officials set about their check of identity cards and registrations without delay. Once again, the check revealed a very large number of people unable to produce identity cards.'

1943

April 2 – 'In the midst of the greatest war the world has ever seen, the Corps of Royal Marines maintains its high peacetime traditions and standards. The Guards-like atmosphere envelops the barracks routine and training, the magnificent esprit de corps still permeates from drummer-boy to brigadier.'

May 24 – 'Oxford has accepted Plymouth's Wings for Victory Week challenge, and in the forthcoming campaign there will be friendly competition between the two cities, each of which has set itself the target of £1,500,000.'

December 30 – 'When 1943 is viewed in retrospect so far as Plymouth is concerned history will record that the citizens regarded themselves as acclimatized to austerity, toughened to Teutonic bombing, and justifiably proud of their comprehensive war work accomplishments, particularly in the volun-

tary category. In fact, they have learned to take the fourth year of war with a philosophical stoicism worthy of the city's tradition. Early in January Sir William Beveridge spoke in the Central Hall on his much-discussed social security plan. In mid-November, Mr C Attlee (Deputy Prime Minister) reviewed the political situation. For security reasons Plymouth's full quota to the fourth year of the war cannot be revealed now, but suffice to say amid the many wartime vagaries as a naval port and garrison the city will be entitled to very honourable mention from the historians.'

1944

March 10 – 'Mr Hamilton Kerr moved an amendment to the Education Bill in the Commons today that no teacher shall be dismissed solely on account of marriage. Mrs Cazelet Keir said that removal of the marriage bar was a necessity if sufficient teachers were to be recruited to put the Education Bill into operation. It was a bad thing for girls in school to think that teaching was a celibate profession.'

April 26 – 'Preview of Reconstruction Plan for Plymouth – The Old Town of Devonport May Disappear: 'The Plan and models for the reconstruction and redevelopment of the City of Plymouth is provided for in the report of Mr J Paton Watson (City Engineer and Surveyor) and Prof Patrick Abercrombie (consultant planner). It was agreed that the Plan as unfolded was one of tremendous depth and vision. Mr Paton Watson said the amount of blitzed and 'blight' property gave them every justification for proceeding with such a Plan. It provides for an alternative layout for Devonport should the Admiralty scheme for the expansion of the Dockyard become abortive.'

May 3 – 'There has been precious little time in this garrison town to dream or see visions, but where there is no vision the people perish.' J Paton Watson.

June 6 – 'The Allies have established beachheads in Northern France … the landings were made in Normandy between 6 a.m. and 8.15 a.m., mine sweepers clearing a way …'

1945

May 8 – 'World-wide thankfulness is evoked by VE Day which has brought to an end this destruction of human lives after nearly six years. Tonight the King will broadcast to the Empire and the world. Today and tomorrow are regarded as public holidays, in which Plymouth shares joyfully with other cities which have felt the brunt of the war.'

May 16 – 'Victory celebrations in Plymouth last week resulted in licensees doing a record trade as long as supplies lasted and also losing a record number of glass-es. One estimate of the trade done before the celebrations ended was that it was in the neighbourhood of £120,000.'

August 15 – 'Peace, hidden for nearly six years amid the swirl and devastation of bestial war, today once more assumed dominion over the world and received the heartfelt acclamation of suffering humanity, Japan, the last enemy, weeping and 'deeply apologizing to its humble Emperor,' has ended days of vacillation by accepting unconditional surrender. With the last stroke of midnight, the bonds of war snapped. Peace. In Plymouth the Hoe, that great historic spot where through centuries Plymothians were wont to gather for great occasions, was the focal point; at Devonport it was the high ground of the park.'

December 17 – 'Eight naval ratings were drowned when a motor launch in which they

CHURCHILL's National Government had been tardy in designating Plymouth an evacuation area: 12,000 children were eventually moved out into the already evacuee-crowded towns and villages of Devon and Cornwall.

QUEEN Elizabeth (later the Queen Mother) inspects WRNS at Devonport early in 1942. Right, later in the same year Tavistock girls danced away the wartime blues.

▼ *PLYMOUTH buried many who had died in the blitz in a communal grave at Efford: the coffins were draped in Union Flags. Not all the bodies were identified.*

were being taken ashore from H.M. Minesweeper Tenby during a gale at Plymouth last night was swamped and sank.'

1946

November 2 – 'Devonport's part in the great contribution of the Royal Dockyards in waging the war at sea is revealed in an official Admiralty report issued today. Tribute is played to the part played by all Royal Dockyards, and Devonport is singled out for special praise for its handling of the maintenance and repair of many of the big ships of the Royal Navy. The report states that although most of the ships engaged in the Battle of the Atlantic were repaired in commercial shipyards, over 200 destroyers were repaired or refitted in Devonport in the first 18 months of the war. The Dockyard also refitted and modernized ten battleships and many cruisers. Outstanding was the work done on the cruiser H.M.S. Belfast. The Dockyard gave much assistance to civilian authorities who had to deal with the consequences of very heavy air raids on Plymouth. It planned and helped to equip the Royal Naval Air stations at Yeovilton, St Merryn, Henstridge, Culdrose, Arbroath and Crail, as well as armaments depots at Ernesettle and Trecwn. The Dockyard itself suffered extensive damage from air raids but recovered 90 per cent of its former efficiency within two months of the last and heaviest raid.'

WARTIME fuel shortage helped breathe the kiss of life into Plymouth's last trams which lingered on until autumn 1945.

November 12 – 'Despite the promise of Food Minister (Mr John Strachey) that iced Christmas cakes will be available this year, Plymouth housewives are to be disappointed. Plymouth master bakers pointed out, despite promises, that the Food Ministry had made no allocation of essential ingredients – fat and fruit.'

November 25 – 'War Office and Admiralty requirements on Dartmoor total some 70,000 acres. The danger of unexploded ammunition meant no public access would be possible to some 52,000 acres.'

December 16 – 'Princess Elizabeth & Greek Prince: 'Although reports of an engagement between Princess Elizabeth and Prince Philip of Greece have been denied by Buckingham Palace, the New York Times splashed the story on its front page today.'

December 20 – 'With a population of 30,000 they had a right to expect Devon County Council to provide a maternity hospital in the area, said Mr J Finnigan at Plympton St Mary Rural Council.'

December 20 – 'Plymouth Furnished Houses Rent Tribunal reduced rent for a naval tenant at St John Street, Devonport today for two attic rooms from 42s to 17s.1d (86 pence) a week. Water supply was in the yard and he had to go down 90-odd steps to reach it. Water came through the roof and down the walls. He did not have a front door key. If it was known he was coming ashore the door was left unlocked otherwise he had to knock someone up. The landlord did not consider the rent too dear, and said he was only trying to make a living.'

December 28 – 'Loaded up with gas bombs and high explosives, unused relics of the war which cannot safely be destroyed by any other means except drowning, the 4,971 steamer Empire Lark will shortly be towed out to sea from Millbay Docks, Plymouth. Hundreds of miles from shore stop cocks will be opened and the ship will be sent to the bottom with her terror cargo.'

1947

January 30 – 'Today the Westcountry lies buried under the heaviest fall of snow for fifty years. Plymouth City Meteorologist reported this morning: Snow, average depth 12 to 14 inches, temperature 28.6 F. The last heavy fall of snow was on February 15, 1920, when the depth was about 9 inches. Over 4,000 employees of Devonport Dockyard residing in outlying districts were unable to get in to work today. This number included the whole of the Dockyard 'village' at Lee Mill. Almost all outside work was at a standstill in the Dockyard. Over 1,000 men are being employed by the City Engineer's department in clearing the main city streets and shopping centre. Householders opened their doors and stepped out into the snow – up to their knees.'

March 13 – 'Westcountry traders and those already planning their holidays this year are alarmed at the Government decision to cut passenger services by 10 per cent this summer and also to suspend the famous 'Cornish Riviera'. The cuts are necessary to conserve coal and supplies over the Easter holiday.'

March 17 – 'In Raleigh-lane, Plymouth today, five men made history. Corporation workmen at 8.15 a.m. drove their picks into the road to begin reconstruction of the City Centre. They were tackling the drainage system before the start of the east-west road.'

October 2 – 'The first post-war launch at Devonport Dockyard will be notable for the fact that it will be half a ship and she will go down to water bow first. Construction of the 13,000-ton tanker, Archduchess is rapidly nearing completion. A victim of mine warfare, only the stern half of the vessel was salvaged and consequently towed to Devonport.'

October 28 – 'Plymouth accorded a tremendous welcome to the King and Queen this afternoon when their Majesties gave a Royal inauguration to rebuilding the war-devastated city. The King unveiled a bronze tablet commemorating the start of the ambitious project – the first major work of reconstruction in the country arising from war damage – and officially named the two great roads of the future, Royal Parade and Armada Way.'

October 27 – 'The intensive raids on Plymouth in March and April, 1941, were the result of the Nazis' dissatisfaction with the bombing up to February, and their desire to eliminate naval bases such as Devonport, which they regarded as being vital to Britain's successful prosecution of the war. This is revealed by remarks of Grand Admiral Raeder, Commander-in-Chief of the German Navy in a report to Hitler as shown in the 'Fuehrer Conferences on Naval Affairs, 1941' published by the Admiralty

last night. Hitler concurred with the report and stated: 'Britain's naval and merchant vessels must be the main targets for attacks. Aerial photographs of attacks on Portsmouth, Plymouth and Cardiff show how ineffective the night attacks were. Attacks on the shipyards in the Tyne and Clyde areas, in Barrow and in Chatham and Devonport are especially important. Ships afloat must be the target of the submarines, ships in harbour must be the target of the Air Force.'

1948

January 17 – 'Centrally-heated blocks of flats, with those on the ground-floor having garden or grass on three sides are envisaged in the redevelopment plan of Union-street (Octagon to Stonehouse Bridge) which was

FIRE gutted the city's St Andrew's, which became a 'garden church' for the remainder of the war.

personally presented by Louis de Soissons, the eminent architect, to Plymouth Housing Committee. The scheme for the first housing redevelopment area in the city, providing for 292 flats and shops and giving accommodation to 1,307 people, pays attention to the needs of the housewife, with kitchens of southern aspect. It makes a special point of privacy.'

January 22 – 'Nobody who cares for the Royal Navy and its traditions can have heard without sadness of the passing of the Queen Elizabeth, Valiant, Nelson and Rodney and the battle-cruiser Renown. It is impossible not to sympathize with the feeling expressed in the House of Commons that some means might be found of retaining them in some way.'

June 30 – 'Plymouth has not yet experienced the marked decline in the selling price of houses reported from other parts of the country. Local auctioneers reported no appreciable difference. Foulston, a semi-detached house at Wilderness-road, Mannamead, was withdrawn at £5,250. A five-bedroomed house, 8 Woodside, Crapstone, offered by Messrs Viner, Carew was withdrawn at £3,500 but subsequently sold privately for £4,030. The same auctioneers sold Merrivale, Great Berry-road, Crownhill for £3,000. No. 32a Cardinal-avenue, St Budeaux sold for £1,155 and 83 Cotehele-avenue, Keyham with vacant possession of three rooms for £870.'

1949

January 1 – 'Shell-scarred H.M.S. Amethyst brought her officers and men home to a great Westcountry welcome today when she berthed alongside in Devonport Royal Dockyard to receive Admiralty and civic tribute for the gallantry and fidelity to duty in the Yangtze shelling. All ratings proceeded on immediate leave following Plymouth's civic luncheon. Amethyst proudly flew the White Ensign she carried in defiance of Communist guns when making her thrilling 140-miles night dash to freedom down the

IN OCTOBER 1947 King George VI and Queen Elizabeth 'opened' Royal Parade and Aramade Way in a ceremony that was a milestone on the city's road to recovery.

Yangtze River. This ensign will drape the memorial to be unveiled in the Royal Naval Barracks to those who lost their lives in the shelling and will subsequently take a place of honour in the Church of St Nicholas.'

September 17 – 'Devonport Dockyard civilian non-industrial staff will be affected by an Admiralty order calling for cuts of 5 to 12½ per cent in the interests of national economy.'

September 29 – 'It will be at least five years before there is any hope of a television service for the Westcountry, according to Mr Herbert Morrison. More populous areas are to be served first.'

November 8 – 'Plymouth City Council decided to promote a Bill in the next session of Parliament for extension of the city's boundaries to include Bickleigh and Tamerton Foliot.'

November 8 – 'The most crowded area in Cornwall was Torpoint, with 4.2 people to each house. The Falmouth average was 3.8.'

1950

February 1 – 'Two new blocks of buildings which together are costing more than £500,000 are now taking shape at the Royal Naval Engineering College, Manadon. These represent the second phase in the development of Manadon as a Naval university for mechanical engineering and its associated technologies. The first College, made necessary by the advent of steam, was completed at Keyham in 1880. The site was too small for expansion and in 1936 the Admiralty bought the fine, 100-acre country site at Manadon with Manadon House, an early 17th century building for which Inigo Jones may have been the architect.'

February 9 – 'A suggestion that there might now be certain restriction of the Admiralty proposals to extend Devonport Dockyard was made last night by Ald Sir Clifford Tozer, chairman of the Plymouth Reconstruction Committee: the Admiralty will definitely take over, as originally intended, a very large area, but unofficially I understand there is now a possibility that there will be certain restrictions, he said.'

February 21 – 'Lady Astor faced a hostile crowd at a Conservative meeting at Paddington Town Hall last night. Hundreds were shut out. When a woman asked: Aren't you a very wealthy family? she replied: The Astors are very rich. Don't you wish you were? ... I would give the last drop of my blood to save this old country from Socialism. A section of the crowd began singing the Red Flag. Immediately Lady Astor began singing, God Save the King, at the top of her voice.'

February 22 – 'Liskeard Borough Council was told last night that there were still 124 families on its waiting list and that some Liskeard houses were no better than mud huts.'

February 23 – 'Mr G Bryn Jones, national president of the Federation of Retail Newsagents, Booksellers and Stationers, yesterday told the Devon and Cornwall Council of the Federation at Plymouth that his delivery boys had later become vicars, teachers, mining and electrical engineers, or gone into business as shopkeepers themselves. In 14 years as a Magistrate he had never had before him any boys who had been thus usefully employed.'

LTD CDR John Kerans and crew members of HMS Amethyst inspect Drake's Drum, displayed in honour of their endeavour and bravery, in November 1949.

February 25 – 'Plymouth City Council will consider a report on Corporation-owned properties in the Barbican area which indicated that 59 properties, involving 115 tenancies are owned by the Corporation, and that it is proposed to consider the demolition or closing of 20 of them: 80 of the 115 families concerned wish to remain in the Barbican area ...'

February 28 – 'A sailor escaped to safety by crawling along a nine-inch ledge 53 feet from the ground during a fire in the early hours of this morning at the Royal Sailors' Rest (Aggie Weston's) Albert Road, Devonport ... about 100 naval ratings were staying at the Rest, but there were no casualties ...'

1951

October 1 – 'Workmen repairing war damage in the dance hall of the Virginia House Settlement, Plymouth, on Saturday, found three strange brick mounds a few inches below floor level. The mounds interfered with the laying of the new floor so the men started to demolish them. A few blows with a pick forced a hole in one and, peering through, the men were startled to see two coffins lying on brick ledges in the gloomy cavity. One of the men lowered himself into the vault and found the coffins rotten with age. A skull in one of them fell to dust when he tried to pick it up. Two other mounds were also found to be the roofs of burial vaults. The second contained two coffins and the third, sunk deeper than the others, appeared to house at least three caskets. Their presence is explained by the fact that the hall was once Batter-street Congregational Church, and the vaults, each measuring about 9ft by 6ft were probably constructed during the church's early history … the church was built in 1704. It 1923, it was closed and sold to Lord Astor to extend the work of what was then the Victory Club …'

October 1 – A Citizen's Diary: 'Any day or evening now as you pass through Bank of England-place, Plymouth, you will see numerous cars with a piece of yellow paper slipped behind their windscreen wipers. This represents the Corporation's latest technique in extracting sixpenny parking fees from motorists. And a pretty poor technique it is. What an imposition … is this not carrying parking facilities to a farcical point?'

December 24 – 'Jack and Jill hold high revel in Emile Littler's pantomime which opened at the Palace Theatre, Plymouth, on Saturday. It is a very pleasant affair indeed with lively music (no moaners, no screaming saxophones, no blaring accordions), delightful costumes, settings and lighting and much fun for the children …'

December 31 – 'Reference to a B.B.C. proposal to erect a 750ft. television mast on North Hessary Tor, near Princetown, to serve Plymouth and the surrounding area - one of the five medium power stations which its is planned to build after the removal of Government restrictions, possibly in 1954 – is made in the current report and newsletter of the Dartmoor Preservation Association. It is known that B.B.C. representatives have visited the South-West to initiate long-term planning for the television service, and though several sites are under consideration no definite selection has yet been made … '

BARBICAN folk lost no time, once the war was over, in re-opening the waterfront.

49

THE IMMENSELY able but self-effacing Prime Minister Clement Attlee bestrides the deck of HMS Vanguard in Plymouth in May 1948.

December 31 – 'Plymouth's film favourite of 1951 was easily Mario Lanza. This genial new singing personality headed the Royal Cinema's list of box-office successes with The Great Caruso. Westerns remained constant in popularity. Plymouth people like the wide-open spaces – they aren't keen on drawing-room satire and sophistication. Although not a first-run cinema, the Plaza's year was interesting because of the public reaction it tested in two directions. The notable re-issues and experiments with foreign films (Jour de Fête, Clochemerle and Bitter Rice) met with a ready appreciation.'

1952

February 14 – 'The number of indictable crimes (in Plymouth) has increased by no fewer than 798 the highest figure ever recorded in the city. Offences under all headings dealt with during the year numbered 3,273 as against 2,475 in 1950.'

February 15 – 'Vast, silent crowds stood bareheaded along the route as the body of King George VI was taken today from Westminster Hall to Windsor to be buried in the shrine of Kings. During the lying-in-state, 305,806 people passed the catafalque.'

February 27 – 'The overall strength of industrial and non-industrial workers in H.M. Dockyard, Devonport is about 16,000.'

February 27 – 'The Lord Mayor of Plymouth (Ald Randolph Baker) said last night there was a crying need for a new theatre in the city.'

August 16 – 'Messrs Ivory and partners, the city meteorologists, said yesterday's rainfall of 2.55in was the highest day's rainfall on record in Plymouth. The previous highest rainfall recorded was 2.27in on November 17, 1916 …'

August 18 – 'More than 30 people are now feared to have died in the flood-battered area of North Devon holiday coast where, during the night, there were further falls of rain. It will be some time before it is known what the effect of this rain will be on the swollen River Lyn, which, after Friday's cloudburst, swept through the village of Lynmouth devastating everything in its way …'

1953

June 3 – 'There was a fairly brisk demand for Coronation stamps at Plymouth post offices this morning. The stamps which are double the size of the normal stamp bear in three cases almost identical portraits of the Queen wearing her diadem.'

August 19 – 'If all goes well 2.237 acres of land in Torpoint's centre will be cleared to make way for ambulance and fire stations and a police headquarters.'

IN 1944 Queen Anne's Battery (now a marina) was still occupied by American servicemen.

August 19 – A Citizen's Diary: 'They say hope springs eternal. It certainly does in the heart of Mr E.F.H.Davey, part-owner of the blitzed Grand Theatre in Union-street. He has been trying to secure a licence for the rebuilding of his premises for some time. The theatre, with a seating capacity of 1,500, was badly damaged by incendiary bombs in 1941, and the dressing-rooms were almost burnt-out. Since then it has been used by a furniture-manufacturing company. Repair work would take about six months. Built in 1889 it is remembered by many older Plymothians for its presentation of 'blood and thunder' melodramas. Among the famous artists who trod its stage, the largest west of Bristol, were Sir Henry Irving, Charlie Chaplin, Gracie Fields and Randolph Sutton. From 1936 onwards it was used as a cinema … '

▲ *LEICESTER Harmsworth Hous?, left, with clock, miraculously survived the fiery inferno of April 1941, emerging almost unscathed to become a distinctive feature of the post-war city centre streetscape.*

▼ *The BUILDING which was home to the Herald from its birth until the move to Derriford in 1992.*

August 19 – 'England beat Australia by eight wickets at the Oval this afternoon and so regained the Ashes which they lost as long ago as 1934. Compton made the winning hit and thousands of people invaded the pitch.'

1954

January 1 – 'It was in 1754, two centuries ago, that the parish church registers recorded the baptism of Bligh, of the Bounty fame. Captain Bligh, stern disciplinarian, but good sailor withal, was of old Cornish stock.'

January 1 – 'The honour accorded Mr V.G. Shepheard makes him the fourth ex-Devonport (Dockyard) apprentice to receive a knighthood. Former Devonport students to win such a distinction were: Sir William White (Devonport born), Sir Arthur Johns (Torpoint) and Sir Charles Lillicrap (Plymouth). The Rt Hon Leslie Hore-Belisha, M.P. for Devonport 1923-1945; Minister of Transport 1934-1937; Secretary of State for War 1937-1940; member of the War Cabinet 1939-1940; Minister of National Insurance, 1945. Created Baron for political and public service.'

October – 'The Reconstruction Committee considered schemes for providing living accommodation over shops in the neighbourhood of the new pannier market. They incorporate 43 shops with 34 three-storey flats over, and 42 two-bedroom flats of four storeys. Two Plymouth City Centre buildings, the second section of the giant Plymouth Co-operative Society Emporium, and Radiant House, headquarters of the South Western Gas Board, are now under construction.'

October 25 – 'The death has occurred of Mr F.C.F. Cole, who was City Librarian for 20 years, including the war years when the Central Library and 75,000 books were destroyed, and Mr Cole had the colossal task of re-establishing the service.'

WATERSIDE communities such as Morice Town, Devonport, entertained themselves and others with regattas: the greasy pole competition always pulled crowds – June 1950.

1955

January 4 – 'A recommendation that land at Saltash Passage should be leased to the Admiralty was criticised at yesterday's Plymouth City Council meeting. To allow the Admiralty to have land on lease was dangerous, said Mr Stanley Goodman, who then quoted, amid laughter, 'Nil terram nihil nauticus,' which he translated as, 'Never let a sailor pinch your slip.'

January 7 – 'The total number of unemployed in the South-Western region on December 6 [1954] was 17,088 – 10,888 men and 6,200 women – an increase of 659 on the previous month and giving a percentage rate of unemployment of 1.6 compared with a figure of 1.2 for the country as a whole.'

April 14 – A Citizen's Diary: 'Two sparrows in Biblical times, we are told, were sold for a farthing. In 1955 the tiny coin still has a value. Four farthings soon add up to a penny, and a lot can be done with a penny. In the Market the other day I bought a book, it was probably tenth-hand, worth for me more than the penny I gave for it. Now I see brand-new slot machines selling chewing gum to youngsters for a penny, and I have been reminded that one can still cross the Tamar on a ferry for a penny.'

52

THEY stretched in never-ending line … the splendidly utilitarian prefabs, which long defied their anticipated life expectancy in Plymouth.

THE FREEDOM of Plymouth was conferred in 1955 on the Royal Marines with pomp and ceremony on Plymouth Hoe.

April 14 – 'Plymouth hairdressers are apparently taking no notice of the recommendation passed by the National Hairdressers' Federation conference at Brighton on Monday that the minimum charge for a man's haircut be two shillings (10 pence). Plymouth hairdressers already charge two shillings.'

1956

November 6 – 'Among hundreds of Guy Fawkes effigies burnt during celebrations in Plymouth last night was one of Col Nasser.'

November 27 – 'When a police inspector visited Plumer Barracks to make inquiries, he found a group of boy soldiers had decided to go to the Hoe and seek reprisals on Teddy Boys.'

December 1 – 'Over 120 past and present Plymouth boxers gathered at the Magnet Restaurant, Plymouth, last night for what was described as a unique meeting in the annals of British boxing. The occasion was a reunion dinner and social event at which many of the boxers and spectators of the old Cosmopolitan Gymnasium gathered to honour the former promoter, Mr Harry Jenkins.'

December 3 – 'Mr Leslie F Paul, chairman of the Port of Plymouth Chamber of Commerce, said if financial consideration made it impossible for the Tamar Bridge and the Plymouth Civic Centre to be developed together, the bridge must be given first priority.'

December 7 – 'Graphic stories of the Port Said landings were told in Plymouth today when the aircraft-carrier Ocean arrived in the Sound. On board were 600 men of 42 Commando, Royal Marines, 200 of the Royal Artillery and a few R.A.F. men … '

December 20 – 'Proposed increases of up to 4s (20 per cent) in the basic rents of Plymouth Council house dwellings have been announced. The Council has nearly 17,000 tenants.'

NAVY Days, 1956.

1957

January 15 – 'From 1939 to 1956 Plymouth received from the sale of salvage, waste paper, metal and kitchen waste, a sum of £1,010,024. Kitchen waste represented £750,000 of the total.'

January 31 – 'Not yet seven years old, Plymouth's largest housing estate (Whitleigh) will have 2,200 dwellings and a population of 10,000 people when major housing development ends this year.'

September 10 – 'Plymouth's new Head Post Office was opened today. The £150,000 structure is the first of its size and importance to be opened in Britain since the war. In the 16th century there was a weekly post from Plymouth to London by stage coach, then a three-day journey. The first Post Office was established at Devonport in 1793. In 1812 a postman went through the town ringing a bell between 3 p.m. and 4 p.m. to collect letters.

A sorting office was established after the amalgamation of the three towns. The Head Post Office in Westwell-street was destroyed by enemy action in 1941. Business has been carried on from the cramped building in Drake-circus which closes tonight.'

September 20 – 'H.M.S. Fisgard, the artificers' training establishment at Torpoint has had 160 cases of 'flu: in H.M.S. Raleigh, the total of cases since the outbreak began was 236.'

September 28 – 'The new Plymouth factory at Whitleigh by Messrs C and J Clark, the Somerset shoe manufacturers will be producing 12,000 pairs of shoes a week in 14 months' time.'

1958

August 1 – 'A compulsory purchase order made by Saltash Borough Council of 44 properties and sites making up half the historic Waterside area has been confirmed by the Minister of Housing. It paves the way for a second main stage in a big slum clearance.'

October 3 – '£1,475, St Budeaux, Modernised house comprising 4 good rooms, kitchen, bathroom: £1,595, Plympton, 3-bedroomed houses to be erected, 90 per cent mortgages available: £2,100 Plymstock, spacious modern bungalows, fitted with every modern convenience.'

December 29 – '1958 was the year when war-shattered Devonport, neglected for so long, got its first real face-lift. Progress continued on the massive new workshop block of the Plymouth Technical College. One of the most unusual projects begun was the rebuilding of Mount Edgcumbe House. Next May the new 51-shop Pannier Market will open. Demolition of Westwell-street begins next month to clear the way for the great square of the Civic Centre, extension of Armada Way and skyscraper administrative block. In front of the Crescent, a section of road is being built to facilitate the erection of the new Athenaeum. Despite the Bank Rate brake, Plymouth grows; well over 600 houses were completed with 300 more in hand. In the Civic Centre since 1947, 200 shops have gone up. Plymouth Argyle's feat to get to the top of the Third Division filled the hearts of soccer-loving Plymothians with joy. At the end of March, the city's new Breton-side bus station was opened. For Roman Catholics the 100th anniversary of their cathedral was one of the highlights.'

MILLBAY Station (1849-1971. Brunel attended its opening and it achieved a reputation as a rail terminus for the luxury liner passengers: such traffic ceased in 1941.

57

June 2 – 'Devonport's Fore Street was yesterday closed to the Plymouth Corporation buses ending a service of more than 50 years.'

June 2 – 'A Rock 'n' Roll Dance at Plymstock Recreation Hall developed into an unholy brawl with blood flying all over the place and women screaming, Plymstock Parish Council was told. The Council decided to ban rock 'n' roll dances at the hall … '

August 6 – 'Workmen have finished the first important stage of building the suspension bridge to link Plymouth and Cornwall. Hundreds of tons of rock from Plympton quarries have been used for a wide ramp running 75 yards out into the river on the Plymouth side.'

August 7 – 'Plymouth City Council has completed 11,984 houses since the war, and 247 new houses are at present being built in the city. Private builders have constructed 2,643 houses in Plymouth and 108 are under construction.'

August 7 – 'The Home Office said the Prison Commissioners decided against turning Fort Tregantle into a prison or rehabilitation centre. It would be difficult and costly to make escape-proof.'

October 6 – 'As the drought goes on and temperatures remain in the unseasonable 70s, the water supply situation in parts of the Westcountry worst hit is described as desperate.'

◀ *PHOENIX arisen: Plymouth City Centre reinstated.*

September 12 – 'One of the first cars in Plymouth to undergo the Ten-plus examination for older cars was driven on to the ramp at a city garage today. An hour later the owner was driving off with his Pass certificate. His 14-year-old car had been well looked after.'

September 16 – 'The Minister of Housing and Local Government has refused permission to anchor vessels in Stonehouse Pool for use as a helicopter station.'

September 19 – 'Alma Day was celebrated at the Royal Citadel, Plymouth, on Saturday with a pageant and display which spanned 200 years' history of the battery of 29 Field Regiment R.A.'

September 19 – 'Teams from the three women's services will take part in next year's Ten Tors tour over Dartmoor – the rugged, two-day. 55-mile trek which service teams and civilians make to qualify for medallions and certificates. The (first) awards were presented at Rawlinson Barracks, Denbury on Saturday.'

September 19 – 'H.M.S. Beagle is to leave Plymouth tomorrow to retrace part of the voyage made by Darwin in 1831 … '

September 22 – 'The possibility of Plymouth sponsoring a university was mentioned in a lecture at the Swarthmore Settlement, Plymouth, last night. Prof. John Lawlor, Professor of English at the University College of North Staffordshire at Keele who was educated at Devonport High School for Boys said that if a university were sponsored locally it would imbibe the character and purpose of the locality.'

September 22 – 'A scheme that will replace one of Plymouth's worst slum areas and, when completed, will be an example of planning for the whole country, was approved yesterday. It is the joint plan of the City Architect and the City Engineer for the redevelopment of Devonport's Ker Street area. The scheme, including the building of three 16-storey blocks of flats, will result in accommodating 1,200 families, 270 of them in tower blocks.'

November 9 – 'Cornwall County Council was told at Truro yesterday that the new County Hall was going to cost at least £120,000 more than ratepayers had been led to believe. Since the decision to spend £650,000 on the new building, proposals have been put forward for the inclusion of a Civil Defence and W.V.S. headquarters.'

November 9 – 'Stonehouse's prehistoric limestone caverns, discovered in the 18th century and since lost to modern knowledge have, it is believe, been rediscovered by builders excavating foundations for a new warehouse in George Street. Directing a pneumatic drill into limestone boulders, a workman found the rock giving way to expose a 10ft shaft with two long fissures squeezing from it. Remains of prehistoric rhinoceroses, horses, oxen, deer, and other animals were once found in the caverns but were destroyed when the Athenaeum was blitzed in the last war.'

1961

April 13 – 'Moscow today prepared a gigantic welcome for Maj Yuri Gagarin, the Soviet cosmonaut, who is believed to be at a secret headquarters somewhere in Western Russia giving scientists more details of his round-the-world space flight yesterday. Meanwhile his shy, hazel-eyed wife, Valentina, and their two children await his return to their modest two-room flat, which he left several days ago without saying where he was going.'

April 13 – A Citizen's Diary: 'Primrose gathering for advertising or profit is under fire from those who see in it the possible eventual extinction of the species in the Westcountry's hedgerows and fields. Hundreds of bunches are sent during the season from villages in South Devon, especially from the Totnes area. Prices range from 9d to 3d a dozen. Mass commercial exploitation would be really harmful, but the hardy primrose is no delicate flower. These bunches of primroses undoubtedly brighten many a foggy day in London and other big centres.'

April 13 – 'By 1965, six or eight new £10,000-£20,000 youth centres will be built in Plymouth, if the city's Youth Committee has its way.'

May 18 – 'Deep disappointment was expressed (in Plymouth) last night at the decision by a House of Lords Select Committee that the corporation's Harrowbeer Aerodrome Bill should not proceed. Petitioning against the Bill was Devon County Council along with several organisations. The day will come not only when Plymothians but those who believe in the future of the West of England especially the South-west will regret the decision arrived at by their Lordships (said Ald Sir Clifford Tozer). Mr John Foot, of the Yelverton Residents Association thought the cost to the opposition would be in the region of £8,000.'

August 12 – 'The Westcountry had its heaviest traffic of the year today as the go-home scramble reached its peak and by late morning 20 miles of traffic jams were counted in the Exeter area, with a ten-mile queue along the A38 … from an Automobile Association spotter plane a *Western Evening Herald* reporter saw chaos on the bypass.'

August 16 – 'There is a widespread belief among industrialists in the South-west that Britain's entry into the Common Market would, in the long run, be of benefit to the Westcountry.'

October 24 – 'High winds and driving rain swept the Tamar Bridge early today as the first traffic went across. The bridge has been built to sway a maximum of three inches in a 100-mile-an-hour gale and it did, in fact, move perceptibly. At carriageway level the winds gusted to 60 miles an hour, giving pedestrians an invigorating time – provided they avoided the rainstorms – as they walked along the footpath 110ft above the Tamar.'

October 24 – 'Amid the blaring of car horns, singing passengers and rockets flashing across the sky over the Tamar, the Saltash ferry made its last trip last night. Rockets were fired from the ferry, which was ending 600 years' service between Devon and Cornwall.'

1962

July 3 – 'Plymouth City Council yesterday rejected a proposal to spend £5,000 on a Reg Butler sculpture, 'Figure in Space', for the south ornamental pool in the Civic Centre. Mr George Creber said: 'I do not like it. I do not understand it.'

THE QUEEN MOTHER opens the Tamar Road Bridge in 1962.

THE YOUNG and untried engineer James Meadows Rendel submitted plans for a spectacular suspension bridge over the Tamar in 1822. He had to be content with creating the Laira Bridge (1827) over the Plym. Ironically, his cast-iron masterpiece was replaced two months after the Tamar bridge opened.

July 27 – 'The final scene in Plymouth's day of royal splendour was last night's spectacle of the Royal Yacht Britannia, with her escort of navy sloops and frigates, floodlit in Plymouth Sound as the Queen gave a dinner party aboard. It followed the most comprehensive tour of the city by a reigning Sovereign for many years, the purpose of which was to open the new Civic Centre.'

November 21 – 'The thrice-yearly entry of apprentices into Devonport Dockyard increased the number on the Devonport Dockyard Technical College register from 854 in September, 1961, to 1,001 in May of this year.'

November 23 – 'There are hundreds of young Plymouth couples on an inexorable treadmill. Daily they search advertisement columns. They pound pavements and knock on doors. They are the growing band of flat hunters, young folk with precious little capital and no homes of their own. Flats there are, both furnished and unfurnished, but at a price. And there is almost a complete ban on babies ...'

1963

June 7 – Letters to the Editor: 'I approve of everything Dr Beeching has been doing to run the railways economically. If it was my job, I would scrap the railways altogether and convert them into motor roads for the purpose of carrying heavy freight.'

June 12 – 'Launching a youth centre, particularly one as enterprising as the Ballard Centre in Plymouth, was a more important achievement than launching a rocket into outer-space, said Sir John Hunt, conqueror of Everest, yesterday.'

October 1 – 'Loan sanction has been received by Plymouth City Council for the swimming pool in Central Park. The all-in cost will be £263,000: the approach road is costing £5,100.'

October 9 – 'Finds at Mount Batten tower show that the area was actively used at least from about the 4th century B.C. Relics so far unearthed prove that the Romans came farther West than earlier historians had thought.'

October 11 – 'In the last six months the Tamar Bridge, which reaches its second anniversary in two weeks' time, has carried more than 1,250,000 vehicles. The success of the bridge could will mean that tolls will be reduced yet again.'

November 20 – 'There are now 11,267 applicants on Plymouth's council-house waiting list. This figure compared with 10,955 about five months ago.'

1964

October 19 – 'A reunion dinner was held at the Duke of Cornwall Hotel, Plymouth, last night by members of the newly-formed Old Students Association of the former Plymouth School of Pharmacy. The school was closed last year after 40 years. Mr A.G. Mervyn Madge, secretary of the Plymouth branch of the Pharmaceutical Society, proposed the toast of the association.'

October 19 – 'Members of the Old Plymouth Society who were dismayed by the original drawing of the proposed 13-storey hotel proposed for the Hoe wrote asking the City Council to invite the Art Commission's advice before approving plans for a site so important, both historically and aesthetically. The reply was that the Council had noted the request. A plan reducing the hotel by four storeys was now being considered by the designers.'

October 21 – 'Two further moves in the development of the Plymouth Colleges of Further Eduction are recommended to the Education Committee meeting – the completion of the planned residential nautical college in the College of Technology, and the building of new premises for the College of Art.'

October 22 – 'A hint of a bright future for Devonport Dockyard was given yesterday – at the end of the month contractors would have started work on the first phase of a new central office block in the Albert-road area. Not long ago a bridge was built from South Yard to Morice Yard and only last night steel girders were erected for the final section of the bridge over Ferry-road which will lead from Morice Yard to North Yard. For the first time traffic will be able to go the whole length of the Dockyard without going outside the walls.'

October 27 – 'The trustees and executors of the late Capt. Richard Anthony Meyrick have withdrawn the Drake relics that had been housed at Buckland Abbey from the custody of the Plymouth authorities. The treasures lent to Plymouth 13 years ago for exhibition in Drake's former home include in addition to the drum, Sir Francis's massive ceremonial sword, the world map in silver made by Mercator the Flemish geographer, Drake's silver medal, a bowl with which Drake is believed to have played, and a piece of wood carving from the Golden Hind, as well as some documents of exceptional interest. The relics are being housed in the strongroom of a London bank.'

October 27 – 'The Ministry of Public Building and Works considers 33 St Andrew's Street, Plymouth, not only the best of Plymouth's four remaining Elizabethan houses but of the highest importance of its kind anywhere in England.'

October 30 – 'The average ear-drum took just about all the decibels it could stand when the obviously far from waning Beatles descended on Plymouth in two explosive sessions at the A.B.C. Cinema – their second visit to the city within a year.'

October 30 – 'Work on preparing about a mile of the A38 road between Lee Mill and Ivybridge for a dual carriageway is expected to start at the end of November.'

1965

April 17 – 'Owing to what he describes as lack of official support, Mr James Tannock of Hessenford, who planned to build a new self-contained township at Trerulefoot, between Saltash and Torpoint, has abandoned the idea.'

April 7 – 'The deputy Chief Constable of Blackpool, 43-year-old Mr Ronald Gregory, was appointed Chief Constable of Plymouth by Plymouth Watch Committee this afternoon. Mr Gregory succeeds Mr J.F. Skittery who has resigned because of ill-health ...'

April 22 – 'Swilly, one of Plymouth's pre-war housing estates, is the subject of a move to uplift the area in every possible way. The Housing Committee of the City Council decided yesterday to recommend that it be divided into two parts, one part to be included in Keyham and the other to be known as Trelawney.'

April 23 – 'A warning that the new regional economic planning authorities might restrict local initiative to some extent was given by the Town Clerk of Plymouth, Mr S Lloyd Jones last night. He said it was an appropriate time to look back and see what Plymouth had managed to do without regional planning. Leaving on one side the rebuild-ing of the city, there were two matters which reflected on economic planning. These were the building of the Tamar Bridge and the sending of an officer abroad to attract new industry. Had this local government initiative been used when there was regional planning they might have been told to wait and take their turn, he said.'

April 23 – 'A move by Conservative members of Plymouth Education Committee to delete grammar schools from a list of schools put forward by a sub-committee for a comprehensive education system was defeated yesterday. Labour members said to remove grammar schools from the comprehensive system would be to perpetuate the existing system, and support for Labour's plan came from representatives of religious bodies who are co-opted members of the committee.'

July 29 – 'Westward Television chairman Mr Peter Cadbury announced a trading profit of £293,803, an increase of over £90,000 on 1964. Mr Cadbury said the copyright on the Gus Honeybun puppet was vested in a subsidiary company, Torcliff.'

November 10 – 'When the County Hall Committee of Cornwall County Council stated that it was spending £3,000 on a sculpture by Barbara Hepworth – which the committee said was valued at £9,000 - there were complaints of extravagance. It was stated that only at the last meeting the council turned down an expenditure of £1,000 on rescue equipment for the fire brigade, which would have been used to save people's lives. Ald K.G. Foster, chairman, replied that if posterity judged the County Council on the wishes of some of its members it would be ashamed of having built a county hall not in keeping with the dignity of the county.'

1966

March 30 – 'Caradon Hill, near Liskeard, has been chosen as a site for a B.B.C. 2 transmitting station in preference to alternative sites in Devon because it will reach nearly twice as many people as either of the alternative sites.'

May 25 – 'The first stage of a new district hospital at Derriford, Plymouth, is among those having first priority to start in the Westcountry in the next three years under the revised National Hospital Plan, published as a White Paper.'

September 24 – 'On his two-day fact-finding tour of Cornwall and Devon next week, Mr Edward Heath, Opposition Leader, will be told that the Devonport Dockyard employs 16,000 men and covers 320 acres with two-and-a-half-miles of water front. Wages amount to nearly £13,000,000 a year. In the yard, where over 250 ships have been built, there are 9 frigates, five submarines, one cruiser, three destroyers, one maintenance ship, two minesweepers, one fleet tender, numerous small ships together with our biggest warship, H.M.S. Eagle.'

December 12 – 'A firm pledge that a road would be built to link the South-West with Britain's motor-way system was given by Transport Minister, Mrs Barbara Castle, who opened the Honiton by-pass.'

December 14 – 'The Dartmoor search for the escaped prisoner, 'Axe Man' Frank Mitchell, was called off today when clothing belonging to him was found five miles from Exeter.'

1967

March 9 – 'No change in the rate levy for 50,000 Plymouth domestic ratepayers – but a rise of 6d for those in the extension areas of Plympton and Plymstock which become part of the city on April 1. The pegging of the domestic levy at 11s 4d was made possible by the local Government Act of last year.'

March 20 – 'Appeals for help in fighting the menace of oil from the stricken tanker Torrey Canyon off Cornwall were made by the Ministry of Defence (Navy) today to ports along the Devon and Cornwall coast. A

navy spokesman at Plymouth said the oil slick was now 18 miles long and half-a-mile wide.'

May 12 – 'To the strains of Auld Lang Syne played by the Royal Marines band of the C-in-C, Plymouth, and watched by hundreds of people, more than 300 members of the Plymouth City Police Force today took part in a farewell parade to mark the end of the force as an independent unit. On June 1 it becomes part of a new and larger unit embracing Devon and Cornwall.'

May 27 – 'Sir Francis Chichester was this morning reported 72 miles south-west of the Bishop Rock lighthouse, Isles of Scilly. Gipsy Moth was accompanied by a warship, two B.B.C. ships and an ITV ship. Visibility was poor with fog-patches.'

June 13 – 'A Factory in a Garden is to be built on Plymouth City Council's industrial estate at Estover by the American chewing gum firm, Wrigley.'

1968

April 4 – 'Criticism that Drake's Island Adventure Centre was a luxury and that young people of the city were not getting a fair share of the facilities there were answered by the island's warden. Five years ago (he said) Drake's Island was no more than a rat-infested site, now it was a thriving youth centre which cost Plymouth the equivalent of a fifth of a farthing rate.'

June 7 – For Sale: 'Near City Centre – £1,950 modernised terraced house, 2 bedrooms, 2 receptions, kitchen, w.c., small yard. Peverell – £3,300, terraced house with 3-4 bedrooms, bathroom, 3 receptions, kitchen, in good condition throughout, small garden. Higher Compton – £3,500 compact, attractive, 2-bedroomed detached bungalow with open aspect at rear, in popular area, 2 receptions, kitchen, bathroom, garage space, large garden.'

June 5 – 'Robert Daniel took over the Plymouth Argyle chairmanship last night expressing the hope that the club will be given a chance to start afresh with a new image.'

September 16 – 'Plymouth Corporation, which sends out annually 400,000 letter packets by ordinary mail and 375,000 items at the printed paper rate, is partially to boycott the two-tier postal service which came into operation today. The proportion of letters sent by 5d mail is to be limited to ten per cent but the Corporation cannot avoid the compulsory increase of the 3d printed paper rate to 4d which will put up the cost of issuing rate demands by £1,000 in a full year.'

1969

June 20 – 'TV in colour becomes available to a large part of Devon and Cornwall, including Plymouth, from Saturday July 5.'

June 21 – 'The new 464-acre suburb to be built in the Leigham-Estover area of Plymouth presents a great planning opportunity. The area, separated from the rest of the city by Forder Valley, can be planned to give a sense of unity.'

August 2 – Herald Leader Column: 'Nine years ago the farthing died. Now the halfpenny has gone. It had been in use for six centuries. Within a few years nearly all the old measurements will have gone. Out of sensitivity to its once proud international position the pound will still carry the flag for British currency.'

August 4 – 'The Roman Catholic Bishop of Plymouth, the Rt Rev Cyril Restieaux, laid the foundation stone of the new Roman Catholic Church for Crownhill.'

October 7 – 'The final act in the obliteration of the railway line between Okehampton and Bere Alston has begun. The most famous trains to run over the tracks were the Ocean Liner expresses of 1903-1904 when there was fierce competition to rush passengers and mail to London from Plymouth in the quickest possible time.'

October 7 – 'A new operational base for the support of nuclear-powered Fleet submarines is to be developed at Devonport, it was announced by Dr David Owen, Navy Minister and MP for Sutton.'

1970

May 2 – 'Plymouth Hoe was a kaleidoscope of colour today for the launching of Mayflower '70 – a five-month programme of celebrations. Crowds on the Hoe and in the City Centre, estimated to total between 50,000 and 60,000 added colour and excitement to the occasion. The opening was performed by Senator Leverett Saltonstall, a descendant of a Pilgrim Father.'

May 2 – 'Occupying one of the finest sites in Great Britain, high on Plymouth Hoe, with views across the Sound, the £700,000 Mayflower Post House opened its doors to the public yesterday.'

May 5 – 'Any possibility of pollution by sulphur fumes from the planned oil-fired power station at Millbrook is to be investigated by Dr David Owen MP. Plymouth Employment Committee this week passed a resolution welcoming the power station.'

June 3 – 'In about three weeks the first section of Plymouth's £832,000 North Cross Road complex will be in use – the D-shaped section of the main 280ft diameter roundabout. The Ministry of Transport is paying £566,438 towards the cost.'

June 19 – 'Mr Edward Heath will be Britain's new Prime Minister. Labour's 5½-year rule ended this afternoon. An instant boom gave share prices their biggest ever one-day rise and hoisted the Financial Times index 22.6 points. David Owen kept Sutton for Labour; Joan Vickers strengthened the Tory grip in Devonport.'

December 4 – 'Plymouth and London hope to extend their three-year-old overspill agreement to its maximum capacity by bringing new industry and about 3,000 families to the city from the capital over the next decade. The impetus to expansion of the scheme has

HONOURED – The Freedom of the City was accorded to the Plymouth Command of the Royal Navy Barracks in 1963: the sailors celebrated by marching down Royal Parade with bayonets fixed.

been the conferment on Plymouth of inter-mediate area status and the establishment of the Wrigleys factory at Estover which the Greater London Council has regarded as a pilot for the overspill project. Four of the firms which are planning to come to Plymouth are participating in the overspill scheme – Die Casting Machine Tool Co., the Rodene Timer Co., D.O. and E. Industries Ltd., and largest of all, Arrow Electric Switches, which plans to start with a work force of 700 that will ultimately be built up to 1,000. One advantage of the scheme that may bring about 10,000 new residents to Plymouth from London during the next ten years, is the additional subsidy available on the housing front.'

December 6 – 'After a 17-day hearing over a period of five weeks the Plymouth Corporation and South-West Devon Water Board's scheme to build a large reservoir at Swincombe in the heart of the Dartmoor National Park was rejected by a House of Commons Select Committee at Westminster yesterday.'

December 9 – 'Power cuts throughout Britain soared to a staggering 31 per cent and the Electricity Council pleaded with con-sumers to economise on power. Emergency generators borrowed from the Forces were being installed today by Plymouth and District Hospitals Group to save medical ser-vices from disruption by power cuts. The chronically sick at Plympton Hospital spent most of yesterday without heat or light in a prolonged blackout.'

1971

February 9 – 'The proposed Central Electricity Generating Board oil-fired power station at Millbrook would cost £120 million; its capacity would be 1,320 megawatts and the station would burn two million tons of oil fuel a year accepting weekly deliveries amounting to about 40,000 tons from sea tankers. The chimney would be 675 feet high, and 30 million gallons of water an hour would be extracted from and returned to the estuary for cooling. The Insworke Point (Millbrook) site was first class.'

February 16 – 'Plymouth will be demoted to a district authority under a new administrative county of Devon in the first major reform of local government this century. The city will lose many of its functions, including education, personnel, social services, roads and traffic. This Conservative bombshell is contained in a White Paper presented to Parliament.'

August 12 – 'The Department of Education has given Plymouth the green light to go ahead with the building of a new one million-pound College of Further Education at Kings-road, Devonport.'

August 14 – 'A giant mural showing a group of Elizabethans walking through an alley-way is taking shape on a wall on Plymouth's Barbican. The 50ft by 40ft painting is the work of Mr Robert Lenkiewicz, a Londoner, who came to Plymouth four years ago.'

October 29 – 'Britain's decision to join the Common Market was hailed by members of the Six as a milestone for Europe.'

1972

January 20 – 'The United Kingdom unemployment figures have soared past the one million mark for the first time for a quarter of a century. In the Plymouth area, 5,036 are now out of work.'

January 25 – 'Plymouth's proposal for a Tamarside county was rejected by 19 votes to 5 by the Commons Committee on the local Government Bill at Westminster. Dr David Owen M.P for Sutton said that Plymouth had been betrayed by the Tory Government.'

January 27 – 'Plymouth's own firm of stockbrokers, Westlake and Co., has moved this week to new premises on the second floor of Princess House, part of the Drake Circus development.'

December 28 – 'With the reclamation of Stonehouse Lake now almost complete, the long quest to get a playing field on their back doorstep is nearing fulfilment for two schools, Devonport High for Boys and Tamar Selective Secondary. At one time Stonehouse Creek was a direct passageway for sick and wounded servicemen from ships in the Sound to the former Stoke Military Hospital. The inlet existed until about 1890. By 1905 the lake above Millbridge had been filled in and Victoria Park laid out.'

December 29 – 'The dramatic rise in house prices this year is over, and is unlikely to start again in the foreseeable future, Mr Peter Wilkinson, chief executive of Anglia Building Society said today. He says we have now reached a price plateau and the housing market is experiencing a return to sanity.'

1973

January 2 – 'When the French ferry ship Kerisnel drops her stern door on the new roll-on, roll-off ferryport terminal in Millbay Docks at 7 a.m. tomorrow, Plymouth's front door will be open to the EEC. The first vehicle ashore will be hauling cauliflowers from Brittany to up-country markets.'

January 2 – 'More people than ever lost their lives on the roads of Devon and Cornwall last year. The provisional figure given by the Police yesterday was 213. In 1971, 155 people were killed and in the previous year 164 died … '

January 13 – Leader Column: 'Now that the Government has given up the fight

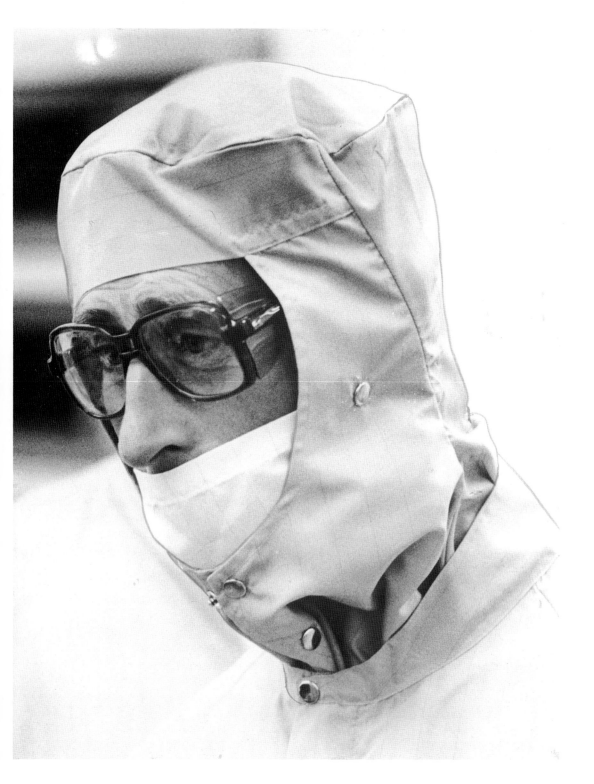

against Dutch elm disease, Plymouth City Council has to decide whether it will abandon the campaign to save the city's 8,000 elm trees.'

January 20 – 'Building of the first-phase of the new Plymouth District General Hospital at Derriford should be started within the next 15 months.'

May 12 – 'Plymouth City Council has been offered a record £216,656 for a half-an-acre of building land on the Hoe – a bombed site between the Berni Grand and Mayflower Hotels.'

August 24 – 'Permission to build a £150 million oil-fired power station at Insworke Point, Millbrook, has been given to the Central Electricity Generating Board.'

1974

April 1 – 'Motorists were out in force yesterday to soak up the sunshine – and petrol at its pre-VAT price.' (50 pence a gallon).

April 2 – 'Cornwall could be the site for an exploratory borehole to exploit geothermal energy – heat from $2^{1}/_{2}$ miles down in the earth. It is not a Jules Verne fantasy but a serious suggestion to the Department of Energy.'

July 1 – 'There is a strong likelihood that the Tour de France will come to Plymouth again next year. Mr Harold Pattinson, chairman of the Plymouth Tour Committee, said: 'We made mistakes, but if the race comes again we won't let them happen again.' The race has been described locally and nationally as a financial flop.'

July 3 – 'The Breakwater Fort signal station in Plymouth Sound, which was closed

nearly four years ago, has now got a new role as a training area for divers hoping to work in the offshore industry, including North Sea oil exploration.'

July 26 – 'Some would-be home buyers are unable to take advantage of Plymouth City Council's mortgage scheme – because the council says the value of the house should not exceed £10,000.'

August 20 – 'Plymouth is well on the way to financing its own radio station. 'We have had a very good response to our prospectus,' said the chief executive of Plymouth Sound, Mr Robert Hussell, 'towards our minimum subscription of £180,000.'

1975

January 20 – 'Britain's cancellation of the Channel Tunnel project today caused gloom in Paris, and some commentators saw the decision as heralding a British withdrawal from Europe.'

January 22 – 'Oil drilling rigs will be operating off the South Devon and Cornwall coasts within three years – and the effect on both counties is going to be devastating, said a Devon manufacturer who is already involved in supplying the North Sea rigs. He said that a triangular area between Weymouth, Dodman Point in Cornwall and the Channel Islands was believed to be rich in oil and all that remained to be sorted out was what areas will be allotted to the French and British.'

May 13 – 'Planning permission for 233 homes on land at Fort Austin Avenue, Forder Valley Road, Crownhill, Plymouth, was refused yesterday by the city council's planning committee.'

May 14 – 'A Cornish youth who was said to have come to Plymouth on Good Friday with a group of Hell's Angels was fined £100 by the city magistrates today for having offensive weapons – a studded leather belt, a flick knife in the top pocket of his jacket and he carried a length of bicycle chain.'

May 21 – 'Halt inflation, or consumers in the South West Water Authority area will be faced either with intolerable increases in charges of between 40 and 45 per cent, or drastic cuts in the capital programme. That is the warning the chairman of the authority, Mr George Gawthorn, has been authorised to give Mr Anthony Crosland, the Environment Secretary, in London today.'

May 23 – 'Much as expected, the South West Water Authority decided yesterday to go to appeal in the sewerage rate case. On May 5, Mr Justice Phillips announced his High Court ruling that domestic or commercial ratepayers whose properties are not served by main sewers cannot be legally charged a sewerage rate. The ruling stemmed from a court case involving Mr Philip Daymond, the South West Water Authority and a disputed bill for little more than £2. But its repercussions affect 900,000 ratepayers in Britain (200,000 of them in the Westcountry).'

May 28 – 'It's almost here … Britain's first North Sea oil shipment will reach land by the middle of next month … some of Britain motorists will soon be driving their cars on a tankful of home-produced fuel.'

May 30 – 'The public restaurant at the top of Plymouth's 14-storey Civic Centre – an unplanned facility added as an afterthought when the building had almost been complet-

THE HOE has always been a popular venue for major events – here, in 1897 the crowds gather for the feu de joie, part of the Diamond Jubilee celebrations.

ed in 1962 – is to be closed to comply with new fire regulations. In addition, steps are to taken to ensure that not more than 20 people at a time have access to the part of the roof deck open to the public.'

December 27 – 'The lure of the briny reached almost summertime proportions for a time at Plymouth's famous men-only swimming point – the Lion's Den – on the Hoe on Christmas Day, when an extra large number of swimmers had a dip before lunch.'

1976

April 3 – 'Farmers in the Westcountry face a frightening shortage of water because of the continued low rainfall.'

April 10 – 'Plymouth and St Malo are now linked by the cross-Channel ferry Armorique … the new service will complement the existing route between Plymouth and Roscoff.'

April 15 – 'An archaeological assessment of Stonehouse, one of the Three Towns merged to form Plymouth, has disclosed a number of potential finds, including, perhaps, a group of Roman-British tombs. The location of the find is being kept confidential for fear of attracting vandals. Stonehouse contains a number of tangled threads which archaeological skills may unravel.'

April 21 – 'The Environment Secretary is to be asked to agree to the demolition of the Victorian Lloyds Bank building at Derry's Cross, one of the last City Centre relics of pre-war Plymouth, which stands in the way of plans to build a multi-million-pound theatre and leisure complex off Royal Parade. The City Planning Committee decided yesterday that the old bank, a grade two listed building, could not be fitted happily into the complex.'

April 22 – 'The number of out-of-work in the Plymouth area now stands at 9,030. A detailed breakdown reads: Plymouth 4,865 (3,560 men; 1,305 women), Plymouth Careers Office 400; Devonport (including Torpoint) 2,320, Saltash 499, Plympton 417, Tavistock (including Gunnislake) 529.'

July 2 – 'Whitehall has given the go-ahead for the demolition of the 19th century architecturally-listed Nazareth House. The Sisters of Nazareth who had run the building as an orphanage made their position clear. If the conservationists won the fight the Sisters would quit the city, leaving the council to sort out the morass of dry rot, damp and decay behind that deceptively elegant facade. Estimates for restoration work on this, once the Earls of Mount Edgcumbe's Winter Villa, ranged from £5,024 to £32,000.'

August 30 – 'The rain was a very welcome respite but it was still vital to exercise great economy in the use of water, South West Water Authority stressed. Mr Denis Howell, recently-appointed Drought Minister, said it had to rain from now until Christmas to make sure we are all right next year. In Tavistock, people queued at standpipes for their water – in the rain.'

September 25 – 'A floodwater wall of death thundered through an unsuspecting Polperro last night. A life has been lost, people injured, others thrust into deep shock by the tragedy, and properties and cars ruined by the merciless wave of water. The storm, and what it brought, has left Polperro a mini-Lynmouth … '

October 1 – 'The last of Plymouth's flour mills shut this week. For many of Spillers' production staff at the Valletort Mill, Millbay, the closure meant the end of a Stonehouse family tradition in milling. When Spillers announced the intended closure of the 19th century mill – once at the forefront of new milling techniques – it came as a bombshell for the 200 workers.'

LITTLE was left of Plymouth after the blitz – and in 1973 the value of a half-acre bombed site on the Hoe between two hotels was worth a record £216,656. ▶

1977

January 11 – 'An anonymous Westcountryman has offered to pay £75,000 for the Palace Theatre in Union Street, Plymouth, and is willing to spend more than £300,000 on renovations.'

January 12 – 'A tender from the John Laing construction firm offering to build 407 new council homes at Estover (second stage) for £3,637,270 found favour with Plymouth City Council's Housing Committee. Completion is expected within 95 weeks, starting in the spring.'

February 4 – 'Concorde is to blame for the things that go bump in the night above Devon and Cornwall, noise experts said.'

February 4 – 'Police officers at Plymouth City Centre are this weekend preparing for their move to the new £1-million sub-divisional headquarters at Charles Cross, Plymouth. There will be few regrets at leaving the cramped City Centre and Greenbank stations. The opening comes three months after the £1.4-million Divisional Police Headquarters at Crownhill began operations.'

September 23 – 'Foreign Secretary and MP for Devonport, Dr David Owen spent more than an hour touring the new Institute for Marine Environmental Research at West Hoe, Plymouth, yesterday after formally opening the £1.75 million building ...

September 24 – 'Devonport Dockyard's future was now assured, the Foreign Secretary, Dr David Owen, declared yesterday, when he formally opened the yard's £18 million frigate complex.'

1978

March 17 – 'Malcolm Allison, the man sacked by Plymouth Argyle 13 years ago, has been brought back to Home Park in a desperate bid to stave off the threat of relegation to the Fourth Division for the first time in the club's history ... '

March 28 – 'The captain of a Dutch motor vessel was fined £350 when he appeared before Plymouth magistrates today under legislation designed to prevent the spread of rabies ... '

July 28 – 'Energy Secretary Mr Anthony Wedgwood Benn has refused to approve Central Electricity Generating Board's plans for Millbrook Power Station at Insworke Point.'

July 28 – 'Five thousand workers in Devonport Dockyard walked out in the latest pay protest to hit defence establishments throughout the South-West.'

October 14 – 'On Friday the 13th and just eight days before Trafalgar Day, RO5, formerly the aircraft carrier Eagle, was slipped from her moorings in the Hamoaze where she has lain since 1972 and shepherded out into the Sound by six tugs for her final voyage. In brilliant afternoon sunshine six tugs towed the 50,000-ton dead ship meekly past the mainly silent crowds who lined rails and walls from HM Dockyard to Devil's Point ... as fog, the only weather hazard, cloaked the former carrier on her final voyage to her burial ground in Loch Ryan, the dead ship finally died, and H.M.S. Eagle, the legend, was launched.'

FIFTY YEARS A CITY

October 17, 1978 –
'The Plymouth of today bears no comparison with the town that was granted city status 50 years ago. In 1928 the city had a population of about 207,000 and covered an area of 5,711 acres. Today's population is 259,000 while the acreage of the city has increased to just under 20,000 acres. Fifty years ago, one-third of the houses in Plymouth were from 80 to 100 years old, and people were living in residential pockets of great density. In some cases there were more than 200 people per acre. These were slum conditions at their worst for many of the populace, and a problem that the newly-exalted municipalities set

out to solve. In 1928 Plymouth absorbed the villages of Eggbuckland and Crownhill. Then came the war ... the cost of reconstruction has been enormous. In 1939 Plymouth's net loan debt totalled just over £8 million. Today the figure is a staggering £126 million: rateable value has shot up from £1.8 million to £26.8 million. Since 1945 the council has built about 21,000 houses and flats, some 19,500 private houses have also been put up since the war. St Andrew's was restored and rededicated in 1957; the rebuilt Guildhall opened in 1959 along with the new Pannier Market and new Athenaeum. In 1950 Tamerton Foliot and part of Bickleigh Parish were absorbed into the city boundaries, followed nearly 20 years later by the takeover of Plympton and Plymstock in 1967. During the post war period some 50 new manufacturing industries and suppliers have settled in Plymouth, providing jobs for thousands and removing the city's dependence on the dockyard as the one main source of employment for skilled workers. Throughout the reconstruction many interesting and old buildings have fallen victim to the bulldozer. Links with the past were swept ruthlessly away by the onward march of progress. A Saturday night out in the Plymouth of 50 years ago offered far more in the matter of entertainment, relaxation and excitement than the dull emptiness of the city in 1978. There were no less than six theatres to choose from, and to walk down Union Street with its conglomeration of shops, pubs and restaurants was an adventure. It was the heyday of musical comedy which Plymothians adored (and still do). Theatre programmes of that half-century ago offered Coates Gin at 11s.3d a bottle; ladies' shoes from 10s.11d a pair, and at Mumfords a Wolseley Hornet car could be had brand new for £175. Then came the Slump, and those fateful years were epitomised by that act of violence by the council when, in 1937, they demolished Foulston's masterpiece, the Theatre Royal, to make way for a cinema. Worse was to come in the fateful 1940s for

'A SATURDAY night out in Plymouth 50 years ago offered far more in the way of entertainment ...'

by the end of the war only the Palace, battered but alive, and the shell of the Grand were left. Devonport's Alhambra and Hippodrome had gone. Plymouth never really recovered from its former theatrical glory, for the scramble after the war for houses and shops went right on through the 1960s, and no one could be bothered with leisure or entertainment. Perhaps in the next 50 years Plymouth will see the realisation of John Foulston's dream of his leisure complex begun in 1813, the foundation stone of which was unearthed last month, and that once again our city will become a centre for good theatrical shows of all kinds.'

◀ *WATCHING the Tall Ships Race from a splendid vantage point.*

1979

May 8 – '450 staff have moved into the new £2-million sausage, pie and cooked meats factory built for Bowyers on the Newnham industrial estate, from the Beechwood factory in Alexandra Road, Mutley, where there has been a meat-processing plant since 1921. The old factory was built in 1884 as a brewery.'

June 23 – 'Bed-sit land is disappearing from Plymouth. Not for 5 years has the City Council granted any applications to convert properties into bed-sits. Demand is high for single-person accommodation: you can pay £15 a week for one room.'

July 26 – 'The Leicester Building Society forecast that the final rate of house price increases for 1979 would fall to around 20 per cent, and said realism is returning to the market.'

September 11 – 'House prices in the South Hams have rocketed. One estate agent described the market as absolute madness. In Totnes last week, a property which sold for £29,000 had fetched a little more than half of that figure 12 months ago.'

September 13 – 'The National Maritime Museum is to be invited to join Plymouth City Council and the Flag Officer, Plymouth, for talks about a possible maritime museum at Devonport Dockyard.'

September 13 – 'Plans for a new 113-bedroomed hotel at Longbridge, Marsh Mills, have been submitted by Novotel (Plymouth). The proposed site is on land adjacent to the Tecalemit factory.'

1980

May 22 – 'It has had a history of problems, but Devonport Dockyard's new £60 million submarine refit complex will be almost fully operational when Prince Charles opens it tomorrow. '

May 22 – 'The three groups fighting for the South-West ITV franchise today published their plans for the region. Westward TV, which has provided the service for almost 20 years, is being challenged by Television South-West and Westcountry Television.'

May 22 – 'For Sale: 'Higher Compton, semi-detached modern residence, 3 bedrooms, garage, £22,000. Peverell carefully-maintained bay- fronted residence, 2 receptions, 3 bedrooms, modern bathroom, small garden, garage space, £21,950.'

May 28 – 'The average wage in the South West is only £4,700 a year. In Devon and Cornwall it is more like £4,000. With mortgage rates at 15 per cent and inflation at over 20 per cent, how do people cope?'

September 18 – 'Trago Mills boss Mr Michael Robertson has defied a judge's hope that a system of rewarding with cash members of his staff who caught shoplifters should end. He said that at his three stores he lost £150,000 a year through thieving.'

December 23 – 'Unemployment in Plymouth rose to 14,617.'

1981

March 17 – 'Today marked the end of a Royal Navy tradition going back over more than a century – of sailors receiving their pay by having the money placed on top of their caps for all to see.'

April 2 – 'A jobs bonanza could be on the way for Plymouth after the discovery that large-scale deposits of tin and tungsten still exist at an old mining site at Hemerdon Ball, near Plympton.'

July 29 – 'Prince Charles today slipped a gold ring on the wedding finger of his fairy-tale bride, Lady Diana Spencer, to seal, in solemn marriage, the romance which has caught the imagination of the world. It was the experience of a lifetime he had hoped for.'

December 14 – 'It was Iceberg Sunday in the South-West yesterday. On top of blizzards, rain and gale-force winds came crippling power cuts. When the electricity was on, the shivering people could not watch television because of transmitter problems.'

December 23 – 'Letter of the Day: 'How this terrible tragedy of the Penlee lifeboat brings home to me the time when the steamer SS Kentbrook went down on Boxing Day, 1936. Seven men lost their lives, 3 of them Plymouth men, 2 Barbican men, Jim and Jack Glanville and dad, Jack Heveran, Chief Engineer. Mum was left with 6 children and another due in March, and the agony of waiting for news was terrible. Plymouth had a fund and Mum used to send me to the Guildhall every Friday to get £1 from the funds … Mrs J.E. Steer, Plymouth.'

1982

April 5 – '150 Royal Marines received a warm send-off when they left Plymouth for Portsmouth in a convoy of coaches. The Marines were joining the commando assault ship Fearless, due to sail for the Falklands Islands later today. Britain's task force is expected to include many Devonport warships including the frigates Broadsword, Battleaxe, Brilliant, Aurora, Dido, Ariadne and Euryalus, the nuclear-powered submarine, HMS Superb, the landing ships Sir Galahad and Sir Geraint.'

April 5 – 'Plymouth's new register office will be opened tomorrow.'

May 6 – 'The glamour of a West End first night came to Plymouth last night when Prince Margaret was the star attraction in the opening of Plymouth's new £9-million Theatre Royal.'

May 18 – A Citizen's Diary: 'Opposite the Customs House in the Barbican stands a relic of Plymouth's Victorian past. Raised on a granite plinth and towering to more than 20 feet, it is the city's last remaining sewer-gas lamp.'

June 15 – 'The battle for the Falklands is over. Argentinean forces in Port Stanley surrendered at 9 p.m. Falklands time last night, and are being returned to Argentina.'

June 28 – 'Plymouth headmaster, Mr John Pugh, took his 190 excited primary pupils into their brand new £½-million school, Pilgrim Primary. It replaces the 100-year-old Oxford Street School.'

1983

February 2 – 'People in Plymouth's older houses are running the risk of cumulative lead poisoning during the water workers' strike says a top city scientist, by trying to save water without allowing several pints to run off from their taps first thing in the morning to minimise the risk of lead poisoning.'

February 4 – 'Safety fencing along dangerous sections of the A38 between Plymouth and Exeter would work out cheaper than the cost of accidents occurring there. Since January, 1979, 22 people have died on the A38 between the two cities. There have been 450 recorded accidents; in four cross-over crashes alone, six people have died. But Mrs Lynda Chalker, Roads Minister, has argued that the cost of safety barriers could not be justified.'

March 19 – 'A £1½-million development of Plymouth's Queen Anne's Battery at Coxside with a new breakwater giving sheltered moorings is to be considered at the planning control committee.'

June 30 – Over 128,000 school leavers joined 2,983,921 others already out of work: unemployment for the month was 3,112,354.'

December 20 – 'Steeplejacks today began work stabilising Plymouth's collapsed college tower block. The cost of replacing brick cladding on the side of the building is likely to run into hundreds of thousands of pounds. Plymouth Polytechnic director, Dr Michael Robbins, warned that the Poly would be financially crippled if the cost had to come

THE DEVASTATING fire, December 1988, at Dingles, Plymouth.

from its budget.'

December 31 – 'Striking water workers put a damper on everyone's New Year spirits in January as they launched a dispute effectively leaving millions of home without water supplies. Tempers boiled along with the water as office coffee machines went up the spout, tapwater turned brown and raw sewage was pumped into the Tamar … an old man was burned to death in his Granby Way flat but was only found days later; officials admitted that the A38 bridges were crumbling with a concrete disease. In February Prince Charles came secretly to Devon and spent a week mucking – in and out – on a farm. March was dominated by the inquiry into the Penlee lifeboat disaster. April began with a death on board the

Brittany Ferry Armourique; Devonport Hospital was sold to a building firm for housing, though the landmark towers will stay; the Palace was sold to be turned into a nightspot. In May, the city was stunned when two old ladies were found dead with head injuries in Ford Park Road, Mutley ... Plymouth's Theatre Royal achieved a breathtaking loss of £440,000 in its first year. The Queen visited Manadon College in July, a month distinguished by a heatwave and Caradon council hitting the headlines when an angry gunman brandishing a sawn-off shotgun fired into the Council Chamber ceiling before being persuaded to give himself up by Trago millionaire boss, Mike Robertson. That month, a British Airways helicopter crashed into the sea en route for the Isles of Scilly, twenty people on board were killed. In August Devonport Field Gun Crew swept the board at Earls Court while the Saltash Bypass and Tunnel inquiry began ... Princess Margaret's visit to the Theatre Royal to see Annie was preceded by a panic over slack ticket sales.'

1984

February 15 – 'Trident missile submarines could be refitted in a new £150 million purpose-built docking complex in Devonport Naval Base. The new deterrent submarines are planned to replace the Royal Navy's existing Polaris submarines by the early 1990s in an £8 billion programme.'

March 2 – 'One of the first purpose-built centres in the country for training primary school teachers is to be built at the Plymouth College of St Mark and St John at a cost of £100,000.'

March 13 – 'Plymouth Magistrates have been labelled as among the toughest in the country. The city ranks fifth in a league table published today entitled Unequal Before the Law. Radical Alternatives to Prison has identified Plymouth magistrates as among the most potent enemies of civil liberty. In Plymouth 19.5 per cent of men on indictable offences were sent to prison.'

March 30 – 'Mr Peter Levene, Defence Secretary Michael Heseltine's adviser recommended that private companies should possibly take over the management of warship repairs at Devonport and Rosyth.'

May 4 – 'The Royal Marines could move into the doomed RAF Station at Mount Batten when it closes in 1986.'

May 12 – 'Toshiba is to bring another 300 jobs to Plymouth with a £3.5 million microwave oven factory at Belliver.'

June 14 – 'Work is set to start before long on a £274,185 project to save Devonport's historic and mouldering Guildhall so that it can be given back to the people as a community centre. The scheme has attracted an Urban Aid grant of £100,000, the largest of its kind so far in the South West outside Bristol. The work should be finished by November, 1985.'

June 14 – 'A giant 1,000lb World War II bomb was exploded by Navy disposal experts in Plymouth Sound today – 40 years after it was dropped by a German bomber. The five-foot long by two-foot wide bomb was lying halfway between Plymouth Hoe and Drake's Island ... seven hundred men of the Royal Navy's Penguin Patrol arrived home from the South Atlantic today – exactly two years after their victorious battle for the Falklands came to an end. Memories of war were strong as a destroyer and two frigates, HMS Liverpool and the frigates Alacrity and Penelope steered clear of divers recovering the 1,000lb WWII bomb off the seabed.'

August 1 – 'The Government came under fierce pressure from MPs on all sides of the House today to give money to the South-West to resolve the repeated crisis over water supplies. Drought Minister Ian Gow assured the Commons that he would be discussing the problem with the SWWA when he visits the Westcountry tomorrow.'

October 13 – 'If a tunnel was built under the Tamar to replace the Torpoint Ferry the debt charges would be the equivalent of £8 for a return crossing, shocked river bosses have been told. If the cost had to be shared between the Tamar Bridge and the Ferry the equivalent would be £1 extra on a return trip over the Bridge.'

1985

January 12 – 'Plymouth's 20,000 council tenants face shock rent rises of up to £4 a week. The money is needed to pay for next year's £17 million city housing programme.'

January 24 – 'Saltash councillors will fight any attempt by Plymouth to build houses in the town. One councillor launched a blistering attack on Plymouth City Council: They left Devonport in a horrible state and no one in Saltash will allow their town to be turned into a slum suburb of Plymouth.'

February 6 – 'A furious row broke today over a report that Sutton MP Alan Clark referred to Britain's black people as coming from Bongo Bongo Land.'

February 18 – 'Firemen in Devon are proposing a ban on the kiss of life for men because they are afraid of catching the killer disease AIDS. The Cornwall brigade is at present leaving the decision to the conscience of individual members.'

July 5 – 'Delighted Plymouth MP Janet Fookes is on the brink of a personal triumph with the Commons poised to make her kerb-crawling Bill law.'

July 10 – 'Defence Secretary Michael Heseltine made it clear when he visited Plymouth that he is determined to push ahead with his plan to privatise Devonport: 'I am not getting value for money and I will get value for money,' he insisted.'

1986

January 10 – 'House prices in the South West rose by just over nine per cent last year.

Average prices are £28,375 for terraced houses, £42,425 for bungalows and £56,971 for detached houses.'

January 10 – 'The Royal Navy is to sell Devonport-based survey ship HMS Hydra because it does not have enough sailors to run her.'

January 20 – 'Plymouth planners unveiled full details of the £2-million futuristic Hoe Interpretation Centre expected to attract 5,000 visitors a day when it opens in 1989. The copper-domed building will be built on the site of the present Mallard cafe.'

June 13 – 'Most of the residents who claim their lives are blighted by noise and fumes from Plymouth's Parkway have lost their battle for lower rates. Only a third of the appeals were approved.'

June 13 – 'A Devonport Dockyard worker awarded £52,000 in the High Court for a lung disease caused by asbestos said today he had fought the six-year legal battle for the sake of his family.'

June 26 – 'Poverty has increased more than 50 per cent since the Conservatives came to power in 1979. The Child Poverty Action Group and the Low Pay Unit estimate that nearly 11 million people now live on or below the poverty line.'

September 26 – 'Twelve thousand workers walked out of Devonport Dockyard in the biggest protest yet over privatisation plans.'

1987

March 6 – 'Work on the new £16 million Roadford Reservoir dam in West Devon will begin on March 19. The aim is to have the reservoir (to supply Plymouth, South West and North Devon) ready for use by the summer of 1990.'

March 11 – 'Worried Plymouth leisure chiefs demanded that South West Water clean up the polluted beaches in the South West. The east end of Plymouth Hoe failed Common Market clean beach standards. SWW said give us the money and we'll finish the job.'

March 11 – 'Electronic giant Texas Instruments is to close its Plymouth factory with the loss of 320 jobs. The news was described as a severe economic blow to the city.'

August 13 – 'The printing firm, Chase Web, will open its new £15-million factory in October, four months after a huge blaze destroyed its old premises killing three of the workers.'

August 13 – 'Dartmoor Prison governor John May, whose 200 prison officers passed a No Confidence vote against him, admitted that he had been through a bad patch. Yesterday's vote followed five escapes from Dartmoor in the past seven months and a weekend of trouble last month when about 50 prisoners caused more than £1,400-worth of damage.'

December 21 – 'South West Water workers have been told to gear themselves for the privatisation count-down in the New Year.'

1988

January 8 – 'Saltash is poised to become the boom town of the South West. Planners say the prospects for Cornwall's fastest expanding centre have never looked better …

January 26 – 'Angry Saltash residents packed a public meeting in a bid to halt expansion plans for their town.'

January 27 – 'A health authority spokesman said there was an estimated 70 to 90 people in the Plymouth district carrying the deadly HIV virus who had yet to develop the full-blown disease.'

July 5 – For Sale: 'Milehouse – a spacious semi-detached residence £72,500: Peverell – mid-terrace in 'Park' road £58,000: Efford - attractive 1930s semi-detached bungalow £55,950.'

July 23 – 'A glittering Armada Night Dinner welcomed the Queen to Plymouth's historic anniversary … **July 29** – 'Plymouth Sound was turned into a kaleidoscope of colour as a spectacular fireworks display marked the finale of the Armada 400 celebrations. Thousands on the Hoe witnessed the display … the Armada was scattered as golden-lit galleons cruised through the Sound spouting fireworks into the night sky. Massed bands of the Royal Marines played music composed by Devonport-born, Ron Goodwin.'

December 20 – 'Plymouth's prestige department store Dingles was turned into a raging inferno as the city centre's worst fire since the Blitz ripped through the building. Police confirmed animal rights extremists were behind the arson attack.'

1989

April 14 – 'RAF Mount Batten base is to be closed.'

March 4 – 'The cost of Plymouth Domes, originally projected to open during Armada 400 celebrations, has soared to £3.2 million.'

March 31 – 'Dingles was back in business today exactly 102 days after Plymouth's best-known store was reduced to a smouldering ruin in a multi-million pound firebomb attack.'

June 3 – 'Police fear that the killer drug, Crack, is now on sale in the streets of Plymouth and other towns in the South West.'

June 3 – 'HMS Drake celebrates 100 glorious years today with a special open day for Guzz sailors who have passed through the base down the years. The base was originally named the Naval Barracks, Keyham, but some old Guzz ratings will remember it as HMS Vivid. The name was changed to HMS Drake in 1934.'

September 1 – 'Union chiefs at Devonport Dockyard are bracing themselves for news of up to 1,000 redundancies when they meet management for top-level talks this morning … the latest round of cuts is aimed at bringing the workforce down to about 6,500.'

November 10 – 'East Germany threw

◄ *THE HIGH Gothic Victorian Duke of Cornwall Hotel looms distantly and disdainfully over the geometrical architectural jungle of Plymouth Pavilions.*

▲

THE TWIN chimneys at the former CEGB at Prince Rock known jocularly as Eb and Flo crash spectacularly.

open its borders to the West last night starting a jubilant flow of thousands of people. Others danced on top of the Berlin Wall.'

1990

January 25 – 'Winds of more than 110 mph cut a trail of devastation across Devon and Cornwall today. High-sided vehicles were banned from using the Tamar Bridge crossing as the winds caused the structure to sway. In Devonport Dockyard the Frigate Refit Complex was evacuated because of severe damage to its roof.'

January 25 – 'The future of Plymouth's £200-million Quays development today seems in doubt because Burton's are unable to raise enough money for the scheme. It will throw the city's entire shopping strategy into disarray.'

May 29 – 'More than a hundred past and present Devonport Dockyard workers have exceeded the lifetime radiation dose, according to figures released today by Devonport Management Ltd.'

October 8 – 'Devonport Dockyard's training centre is to be axed as part of a cost-cutting exercise. The number of apprentices taken on has been slashed in half over the last four years, in mid-September this year only 75 young people began apprenticeships.'

November 22 – 'Mrs Thatcher resigned as Prime Minister today.'

December 27 – 'Plymouth Sutton MP Alan Clark is to ask for the quick release of Royal William Yard for development. An MoD spokesman warned it could take until 1993 for the Navy to move out.'

1991

January 11 – 'Police patrolling Plymouth city centre late at night are more at risk than beat officers anywhere else in Devon and Cornwall. The greatest risk exists in the Charles Cross sub-division where in the first nine months last year 72 police officers were assaulted. Drink has been singled out as the main contributing factor.'

April 30 – 'Devonport Dockyard is to bid for vital refit work on the Royal Navy's new Trident missile nuclear submarines.'

July 15 – 'Devonport frigate HMS Brave, the longest-serving Gulf War ship, is expected to receive a heroes' welcome when she berths at Devonport Naval base.'

July 15 – 'A rich pageant of aviation history is being recalled today as Plymouth City Airport celebrates its 60th birthday.'

July 18 – 'The jobless total in the city's travel-to-work area of 15,044, takes the rate to 11.7 per cent, the highest since 1988.'

July 20 – 'Detailed plans for the closure of Plymouth's Royal Navy Hospital by March, 1993, have been drawn up.'

December 6 – 'Every South West motorist police pull over will face a breath-test in a major Christmas crack-down on drink-driving.'

December 27 – 'A £1.81 million scheme to remove traffic from the centre of Ivybridge has been shelved.'

1992

February 26 – 'Westcountry TV finally got the go-ahead from the House of Lords yesterday to take over from TSW.'

April 1 – 'The *Evening Herald* has been named Britain's Community Newspaper of the Year at a glittering awards ceremony in London. The *Herald* won the prestigious prize at the National Newspaper Awards gala for its Wake Up Plymouth campaign.'

April 17 – 'Boom times are just around the corner for Plymouth with developers set to spend millions of pounds on projects in the city, former Law Society president Tony Holland forecast today.'

April 24 – 'City councillors have given the go-ahead for two giant supermarkets to be built on either side of Plymouth's Marsh Mills roundabout, despite forecasts of traffic disruption. Sainsbury and Tesco want to start

90

operating by 1993.'

May 19 – 'A Government Minister officially launched Plymouth's jam-busting £24.9 million Marsh Mills flyover today.'

June 18 – 'Polytechnic South West became the University of Plymouth today with staff and students releasing hundreds of balloons bearing the university's new logo.'

August 13 – 'The Royal Navy began its historic withdrawal from Plymouth's Royal William Yard, the first stage in a £45 million land deal that could be a key factor to the city's future.'

1993

January 14 – 'If Devonport Dockyard fails to beat Scottish rivals Rosyth for the right to refit the Royal Navy's nuclear submarine fleet, it will be destroyed.'

January 15 – 'An incredible 10,000 protest postcards urging Prime Minister John Major to give Plymouth victory in the Battle of the Dockyards have flooded into our offices. The mountain of mail will be delivered to Mr Major at 10 Downing Street next week.'

January 23 – 'The future of Plymouth's Arts Centre is in jeopardy because of a cash crisis. Swingeing grant aid cuts planned by Devon County Council would hit its coffers hard.'

March 23 – 'Four Southway School pupils died during a canoe trip between Lyme Regis to Charmouth yesterday.'

March 29 – 'A plan to extend the M5 to Plymouth has moved into the fast lane after Eurocrats published details of a far-reaching transport plan for the 21st century.'

March 29 – 'Every 15 minutes a crime is committed in Plymouth: 15 homes are burgled, 10 cars are stolen every day.'

October 19 – 'Plans to create a new world-beating maritime college in Plymouth have been scuppered by the Ministry of Defence decision to transfer naval engineering training to Southampton. Devonport Labour MP David Jamieson condemned the decision.'

1994

January 11 – 'Ivybridge is the hub of the typical boom family in the South West according to the latest Government figures.'

February 1 – 'Supermarket giants Tesco yesterday ordered contractors to halt work at Marsh Mills, Plymouth.'

March 1 – 'The multi-million lock gates at Plymouth's Barbican are in operation. The gates are part of a £10-million development of Sutton Harbour, which includes a new quayside fish market.'

April 24 – 'The Defence White Paper says the Government is committed to building all four of the Trident nuclear submarines which are to be refitted at Devonport Dockyard from 1999.'

June 2 – 'Dame Joan Vickers, who died last week, and Lady Astor, though belonging to the same party, just couldn't hit it off. Dame Joan complained the indomitable Sutton MP did her best to make a fool of her in public.'

June 17 – 'A year ago the Devonport workforce celebrated securing the £5-billion Trident refit contract – but now they are angry and bitter. DML Managing director Mike Leece said implementing 8,000 job cuts in seven years had been difficult and upsetting.'

July 11 – 'Plymouth today claimed victory in its 20-year battle for independence after the Local Government Commission backed the city's Home Rule demands.'

(Page 88)

◄ *DEVONPORT Dockyard employees fight for the survival of their jobs into the next century.*

SHIPSHAPE – the impressive new building for the Western Morning News Co at Derriford.

Postscript

I FEEL proud and privileged to be Editor of the Evening Herald during its centenary year.

Since April 22, 1895, millions of words have been written in the pages of the Herald. Tales of happiness, sadness and derring-do have filled its columns.

We have recorded major events of the 20th century: two world wars, the General Strike, the development of the aeroplane and the first man on the moon to name but a few.

We have taken thousands of pictures and covered a myriad of local events, many of which have made national news.

The Evening Herald is now looking towards the 21st century.

Our new building at Derriford with its unique design so in keeping with Plymouth's nautical history, is full of computers and the sort of advanced technology even H G Wells would not have predicted in 1895.

We also have a magnificent new press that can print pictures in colour second to none in quality.

The technology may have advanced but the philosophy of the Herald has not changed since that time when the first leader comment stated: 'Our programme is very simple ... it is to give the news of the day in the most readable form ... to provide our supporters with the best halfpenny-worth of reading matter that can be produced.'

I only wish the price was the same!

The Evening Herald will continue to be the voice of the people of Plymouth and its travel to work area. It will continue to campaign and challenge those in authority who try to do us down.

I hope you have enjoyed this fascinating book by James Mildren.

Now for the next 100 years!

Alan Cooper

PLYMOUTH looks to the future – the Royal William Yard (Rennie 1825-1833) lies expectant, awaiting an infusion of new purpose.

CASTLES OF DEVON
by James Mildren
A tour of 16 castles.
'Mr Mildren, whose love for the Westcountry is obvious and contagious, digs out many fascinating nuggets ...'

THE BARBICAN
by Sarah Foot

SECRET DEVON
Introduced by Sarah Foot
Sarah Foot in her thoughtful opening chapter reflects *'... scattered over the county is a strong primordial something ... that makes Devon a secret land.'*

DEVON CURIOSITIES
by Jane Langton

LEGENDS OF DEVON
by Sally Jones

SUPERSTITION AND FOLKLORE
by Michael WIlliams. 44 photographs.
A survey of Westcountry Superstitions: interviews on the subject and some Cornish and Devon folklore.
'... the strictures that we all ignore at our peril. To help us keep out of trouble, Mr Williams has prepared a comprehensive list.'   Frank Kempe, North Devon Journal-Herald

STRANGE STORIES FROM DEVON
by Rosemary Anne Lauder & Michael Williams. 45 phorographss.
Strange shapes and places, strange characters, the man they couldn't hang, and a Salcombe mystery, the Lynmouth disaster and a mysterious house are some of the strange stories from Devon.
'... full of good stories, accompanied by many photographs of local happenings which have mystified'.   Mary Richards, Tavistock Times

GHOSTS OF DEVON
by Peter Underwood, President of the Ghost Club Society

More Bossiney Books . . .

SECRET CORNWALL
Introduced by Madeleine Gould

STRANGE TALES OF THE SOUTH WEST
by Ronnie Hoyle

THE MAGIC OF DARTMOOR
by David Mudd

DARTMOOR REFLECTIONS
by David Mudd
'... a valuable addition to Dartmoor literature.'
June Glover, South Hams Group of Newspapers

PSYCHIC PHENOMENA of the WEST
by Michael WIlliams
The subject of a Daphne Skinnard interview on BBC Radio Cornwall.

MYSTERIES OF THE SOUTH WEST
by Tamsin Thomas of BBC Radio Cornwall
A tour of ancient sites in Cornwall and on Dartmoor.
'... There is little doubt that Tamsin Thomas has become the 'Voice of Cornwall.'
Ronnie Hoyle, North Cornwall Advertiser

CURIOSITIES OF EXMOOR
by Felicity Young
'... a tour in words and pictures of the National Park embracing Somerset and Devon.'
Nancy Hammonds, Evening Herald
'Felicity Young, an artist who has contributed many drawings to Bossiney Books, makes her debut as an author with a beautiful description of Exmoor and its many delights.'
June Glover, South Hams Group of Newspapers

We shall be pleased to send you our catalogue giving full details of our growing list of titles and forthcoming publications. If you have difficulty in obtaining our titles, write direct to Bossiney Books, Land's End, Bodmin, Cornwall.